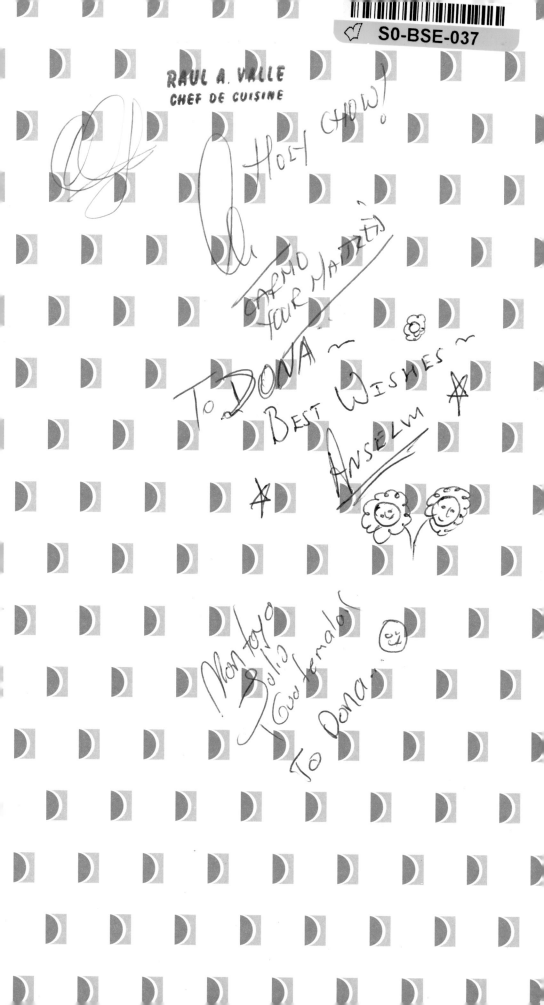

RAUL A. VALLE
CHEF DE CUISINE

HOLY CHOW!

ATFMO
YOUR MADRES

TO DONA ~

BEST WISHES ~

ANSELM

Montoya
Solis
Guatemala

To Dona ~

The Carnival Experience

Dear Guests,

Welcome to *The Carnival Experience*, another fascinating and varied chapter of Cruise cuisine from the Carnival Chefs that will enable you to take some Fun Ship® culinary experiences to your own kitchen.

Filled with more than 100 enticing recipes — many of them requested by you — and dozens of full-color photographs, this cookbook is straightforward with lots of new twists on old classics.

In chapters that cover a wide range of courses and dish types including soups, salads, pastas, risotto, and entrées, the book offers some approachable painstakingly written formulas, which at the same time are easy to understand.

Dessert lovers will not be disappointed, nor will the fitness-conscious as our Nautica Spa®* selection is now even more extensive.

Although some of these recipes demand a cooking commitment, most are as simple to make as they are to enjoy.

Carnival Chefs are proud to share their technical expertise and offer tips on basic ingredients, advance preparation and elegant presentation.

I sincerely believe this book will continue the success of the Carnival Cruise Line Cookbook Series.

I am proud to present the recipes that Carnival's continuing success is based upon.

Bon Appetit!

Peter Leypold
Executive Chef
Carnival Cruise Lines

Contents

Appetizers

Set sail with us to discover a
fascinating array of recipes that
inspire the palate and set the stage
for things to come.

Belon Oyster Ceviche with Beluga
Caviar on Pickled Fennel Roots

Belon Oyster Ceviche with Beluga Caviar on Pickled Fennel Roots

12 fresh Belon oysters, packed in seaweed

2 fennel roots, julienned

¾ cup lime juice

2 tablespoons virgin olive oil

1 bunch chopped fresh cilantro

Kosher salt

4 oz. Beluga caviar

Open the oysters, using an oyster knife. Remove the little muscle (where the oyster is actually attached to the shell). Wash the oysters with cold running water; pat dry. Cook fennel for 30 seconds in boiling salted water; drain. Chill in ice water; drain. Combine lime juice, oil, cilantro, kosher salt and freshly crushed pepper in container with lid. Add oysters and fennel; cover. Refrigerate 45 minutes. Cook seaweed 30 seconds in boiling water; remove. Chill in ice water.

Wash the half oyster shells, pat dry. Spoon fennel salad into each. Arrange oyster on fennel; top with small teaspoonful of Beluga caviar. Garnish with sprig of fennel leaves.

Arrange some seaweed on serving plates; cover with three oysters. 4 servings.

Smoked Chicken Quesadilla

2 cups dried black beans
1 tablespoon clarified butter*
1 lb. smoked chicken breast, cut into strips
½ teaspoon minced garlic
1 teaspoon butter
1 cup corn kernels
½ cup julienned onion
½ cup julienned red onion
½ cup julienned green peppers
½ cup julienned red peppers
½ cup julienned carrots
¼ cup julienned cucumber
1 cup guacamole
2 tablespoons chopped cilantro
3 tablespoons tomato juice
½ cup shredded Cheddar cheese
½ cup shredded Monterey Jack cheese
6 (8 inch) flour tortillas
1 cup salsa
½ cup sour cream
6 sprigs fresh cilantro

Cover beans with cold water; let stand overnight. Drain; place beans in medium saucepan. Cover with 2 quarts water. Bring to a boil; reduce heat to low. Season with salt. Simmer 45 minutes or until cooked through. Let cool in water. Drain. Heat clarified butter in medium skillet; add beans. Sauté briefly. Combine chicken with garlic; season with salt and pepper. Heat butter in large skillet; add corn, onions, peppers, carrots and cucumber. Cook until softened; add chicken. Remove from heat. Stir in beans, guacamole, cilantro and tomato juice. Stir in cheese. Divide filling onto tortillas. Fold into quarters. Heat grill pan; grill tortillas until lightly browned and heated through. Serve with salsa, sour cream and cilantro. 6 servings.

*See Chef's Notes

Smoked Breast of Long Island Duckling

Raspberry Mousse

1 package unflavored gelatin

2 tablespoons chicken stock*

¼ cup raspberries, puréed

¼ cup lemon juice

1 cup whipping cream, whipped

Onion Marmalade

1 lb. red onions, thinly sliced

½ cup sugar

¼ cup Dry Sack sherry

¼ cup red burgundy wine

¼ cup apple juice

1 tablespoon soy sauce

Crushed black peppercorns

3 smoked duck breasts

12 grapefruit segments

6 orange segments

6 sprigs fresh mint

To prepare Raspberry Mousse, sprinkle gelatin over stock in small saucepan; let stand 1 minute. Heat until gelatin dissolves. Cool. Combine gelatin, raspberry purée and lemon juice. Fold into whipped cream. Pour into 6 (2½-ounce) molds. Chill until set.

Place onions and sugar in large skillet for Onion Marmalade. Cook over medium heat, stirring often, until sugar melts and onions are caramelized, about 40 minutes. Add sherry, wine, apple juice and soy sauce; cook until liquids are reduced. Season lightly with salt.

Unmold mousse; dust bottom of mousse with crushed pepper. Place on serving plates. Arrange 4 slices duck, two grapefruit segments and an orange segment in circular shape. Garnish with Onion Marmalade and mint sprigs. 6 servings.

*See Chef's Notes

New England Crab Cakes on Roasted Pepper Remoulade

Roasted Pepper Remoulade

2 medium red bell peppers

1 cup mayonnaise

2 tablespoons chopped capers

2 tablespoons chopped dill pickles

2 tablespoons minced onion

½ teaspoon chopped garlic

1½ teaspoons lemon juice

¼ cup butter

1 tablespoon chopped onion

1 tablespoon chopped celery

1 tablespoon chopped red bell pepper

¾ cup flour, divided

½ cup fish stock*

2½ cups crabmeat

Cayenne pepper, to taste

1 teaspoon chopped fresh parsley

Vegetable oil for frying

2 eggs, beaten

1 tablespoon water

¾ cup soft bread crumbs

For Roasted Pepper Remoulade, heat oven to 450 degrees F. Place peppers on baking dish; roast 10 to 20 minutes or until blackened. Remove; cool slightly. Peel off skin; remove ribs and seeds. Place in blender container; purée. Chill. Combine mayonnaise, capers, pickles, onion, garlic and lemon juice in small bowl. Stir in puréed peppers; chill until serving.

Heat butter in medium skillet; add onion, celery and red pepper. Cook over medium heat until softened. Stir in ¼ cup flour; cook 2 to 3 minutes, stirring constantly. Add stock; cook until thickened, stirring constantly. Add crabmeat; reduce heat to low. Cook 5 minutes, stirring constantly. Season salt and cayenne pepper; stir in parsley. Chill.

Heat oil to 370 degrees F. Shape crab mixture into 6 patties; coat with remaining flour. Combine eggs with water. Dip patties into egg mixture; coat with bread crumbs. Cook in hot oil until golden brown. Serve warm with Roasted Pepper Remoulade. If desired, garnish with glazed lemon slices and peel. 6 servings.

*See Chef's Notes

Jumbo Prawns and Colossal Scallop
with Miso Buerre Blanc

¼ cup urad dal (white lentils)

1 tablespoon olive oil

1 tablespoon chopped red onion

1 teaspoon grated gingerroot

¼ teaspoon ground coriander

¼ teaspoon ground cumin seed

¼ teaspoon ground fennel seeds

Hing powder**

1 sheet nori (seaweed)**, finely chopped

1 tablespoon chopped cilantro

6 baby red beets, peeled

6 baby yellow beets, peeled

1 cup rice wine vinegar

1½ tablespoons sugar

½ tablespoon coriander seeds

4 whole cloves

Minced jalapeño, to taste

Soak lentils for 3 hours in cold water; drain and chop. Heat olive oil in small skillet. Add lentils, red onion, gingerroot, coriander, cumin, fennel, hing powder, chopped nori, and cilantro. Cook until onion is tender.

Cook red and yellow beets separately until just tender; cut into halves. Combine vinegar, sugar, coriander, cloves and jalapeño in medium bowl. Keep beets separate. Pour half of pickling mixture over each; refrigerate until serving.

continued on page 14

Jumbo Prawns and Colossal Scallop with Miso Buerre Blanc
continued from page 12

Red Miso Buerre Blanc

½ cup demi-glace*

½ teaspoon red miso paste

1 tablespoon blood orange
juice or orange juice

1 tablespoon roasted red
pepper purée

¼ cup butter, softened

Grated rind of one lemon,
orange and lime

⅕ sheet nori (seaweed)**,
julienned

6 jumbo shrimp

Togarishi**

1 egg white, beaten

1 tablespoon rose water

1 tablespoon lime juice

6 large scallops

1 teaspoon black sesame
seed

3 stalks lemon grass, cut
into 3-inch pieces

To prepare Red Miso Buerre Blanc, combine demi-glace, miso, orange juice and red pepper purée in small saucepan. Bring mixture to a boil; remove from heat. Whisk butter, a small amount at a time, into sauce. Keep warm.

Combine lemon, orange and lime rind with ⅕ sheet julienned seaweed. Season shrimp with togarishi. Coat shrimp with egg white; cover with seaweed mixture. Heat grill pan. Cook shrimp. Deglaze with rose water and lime juice. Cook scallops. Place one shrimp and scallop on each serving plate; garnish with lentil mixture. Add 2 pieces each of red beets and yellow beets. Surround with 2 tablespoons Red Miso Buerre Blanc. Sprinkle with sesame seed and lemon grass. 6 servings.

*See Chef's Notes

**Available at Asian food stores

Grilled Veal Sweetbreads and Crispy Duck Confit on Wilted Arugula

Crispy Duck Confit

12 tablespoons kosher salt, divided

2 duck legs

1 tablespoon sugar

1 tablespoon grated gingerroot

1 teaspoon cracked pepper

5 cloves garlic

3 sprigs fresh rosemary

3 sprigs fresh thyme

½ cup duck fat

Goat Cheese Fondue

2 tablespoons chopped shallots

1 cup white wine

1 cup whipping cream

½ cup mild goat cheese

¼ cup chopped fresh basil

¼ cup spinach purée

1½ teaspoons chopped fresh thyme

3 whole shallots, roasted

4 tablespoons sherry vinegar

2 tablespoons truffle oil

6 oz. arugula

1 lb. veal sweetbreads

Veal stock

1 tablespoon chopped fresh rosemary

For Crispy Duck Confit, sprinkle 6 tablespoons salt onto duck legs; cover tightly. Place in flat dish; add weight. Refrigerate overnight. Combine remaining salt, sugar, gingerroot, pepper, garlic, rosemary and thyme; add to duck. Cover tightly; refrigerate 12 hours. Turn; refrigerate 12 hours longer. Heat oven to 225 degrees F. Place duck in medium roasting pan; cover with duck fat. Bake 6 hours or until meat falls off the bone. Cut duck into small pieces; reserve duck fat. Just before serving, cook duck in duck fat until crispy.

For Goat Cheese Fondue, combine shallots and wine in small saucepan; cook over high heat until liquid is almost completely reduced. Add cream; reduce to half. Stir in cheese; mix well. Add basil and spinach purée. Season with salt and pepper. Stir in thyme; keep warm.

Roast shallots in 400 degree F. oven until very soft, about 30 minutes. Chop; mix with vinegar and season with salt. Slowly whisk in oil to form dressing. Keep warm. Toss with arugula.

Blanch sweetbreads in veal stock for 2 minutes; let cool in stock. Slice sweetbreads; toss with rosemary and salt. Heat grill pan; oil well. Cook sweetbreads about 1½ minutes per side, do not overcook.

Divide wilted arugula on individual serving plates. Place 3 slices sweetbreads on arugula. Garnish with Crispy Duck Confit and Goat Cheese Fondue. 6 servings.

Eggplant and Zucchini Napoleon

1 large eggplant
3 medium zucchini
½ cup olive oil
2 tablespoons chopped fresh thyme
2 tablespoons chopped fresh oregano
1 teaspoon minced garlic
12 oz. sliced mozzarella cheese
2 cups tomato sauce*

Heat oven to 400 degrees F. Cut eggplant and zucchini into lengthwise slices. Combine oil, thyme, oregano and garlic; mix well. Lightly brush eggplant and zucchini slices with oil mixture. Heat large skillet over medium-high heat; add vegetable slices. Cook 30 seconds on each side. Layer zucchini, eggplant, tomato sauce and cheese in 11x7-inch baking dish; repeat. Bake 10 to 15 minutes or until heated through. Cut into squares. Serve with additional tomato sauce. 6 servings.
*See Chef's Notes

Ratatouille Nicoise with Black Olive Tapenade

Black Olive Tapenade
½ cup chopped black olives
1 teaspoon minced garlic
1 teaspoon capers
1 teaspoon chopped parsley
6 anchovy fillets, minced
Olive oil

1 eggplant, coarsely chopped
2 medium zucchini, coarsely chopped
2 medium yellow squash, coarsely chopped
½ cup olive oil, divided
1 red onion, chopped
1 red pepper, chopped
1 green pepper, chopped
1 tablespoon tomato paste
1 tablespoon minced garlic
3 tomatoes, peeled, seeded and diced
1 teaspoon chopped fresh thyme
1 sprig rosemary, chopped

For Black Olive Tapenade, chop together olives, garlic, capers, parsley and anchovies until finely minced. Add olive oil to moisten. Season with salt and pepper. Set aside.

Toss eggplant, zucchini and yellow squash with salt; set aside. Let stand 20 minutes.

Drain well; pat with paper towels to remove excess liquid and salt. Heat 4 tablespoons olive oil in large skillet; add eggplant mixture. Cook over medium heat until just tender; remove. Drain well to remove excess oil. Add 3 tablespoons oil to skillet; add onion, red pepper and green pepper. Cook until just tender; stir in tomato paste. Heat remaining olive oil; add garlic. Cook until tender. Combine eggplant mixture, onion mixture, garlic, tomatoes, thyme and rosemary; toss to mix. Season with salt and pepper.

Divide ratatouille onto serving plates. Garnish with Black Olive Tapenade. 6 servings.

Crispy Palatschinken Strudel with Chanterelles and Red Onion Confit

Crepes

1 cup all-purpose flour

1 tablespoon chopped chives

1 cup warm skim milk

1 cup water

1 tablespoon vegetable oil

4 egg whites, lightly beaten

1 tablespoon butter, softened

Red Onion Confit

¼ cup sugar

1 cup chopped red onion

1 cup red wine

½ cup sugar

2 cups water

3 firm small ripe pears

3 tablespoons puréed cranberries

½ cup chopped cranberries

Mix flour, chives and salt to taste in large bowl for Crepes. Whisk in milk, water, oil and egg whites until smooth. Add butter; whisk until smooth. Heat medium non-stick skillet over medium-high heat; brush lightly with oil. Pour 6 tablespoons batter into pan; immediately rotate pan until batter covers bottom. Cook until top appears dry, about 2 minutes. Run spatula around edge; turn crepe. Continue cooking until bottom is browned. Repeat with remaining batter. Turn crepes onto waxed paper to prevent sticking.

For Red Onion Confit, heat sugar in medium saucepan over medium-high heat until sugar melts and begins to turn golden. Stir in onion and red wine. Reduce heat to medium. Cook, stirring often, until onion is very soft and liquid has evaporated.

Combine sugar and water in medium saucepan; heat until sugar dissolves. Peel and core pears; cut into halves. Add to saucepan; poach over low heat until tender. Remove from heat; cool. Combine puréed and chopped cranberries; spoon into center of pears.

continued on page 19

Crispy Palatschinken Strudel with Chanterelles and Red Onion Confit
continued from page 17

Chanterelle Filling

3 tablespoons butter
½ cup chopped shallots
1 cup white wine
5 cups chopped chanterelles
2 cups whipping cream
6 egg yolks
1 tablespoon chopped fresh parsley

Vegetable oil for frying
½ cup grated hazelnuts
¼ cup fine bread crumbs
1 egg white
Whole chives
¼ cup sour cream

For Chanterelle Filling, heat butter in large skillet; add shallots. Cook until tender; add wine. Cook until wine evaporates. Add mushrooms. Cook until mushrooms are tender and liquid evaporates; remove from heat. Whisk together cream and egg yolks. Slowly whisk cream mixture into mushrooms. Return to low heat; cook, stirring constantly, until mixture thickens. Stir in parsley; season to taste with salt and pepper. Chill until needed.

Heat several inches oil to 375 degrees F. in deep-fat fryer or heavy saucepan. Place ⅙ stuffing on crepe; fold two ends towards stuffing. Roll up. Make 6 rolls. Combine hazelnuts and bread crumbs. Coat rolls with egg white; roll in crumb mixture. Place in hot oil; cook until golden brown (about 6 minutes). Slice diagonally. Place on individual serving plates. Top with Red Onion Confit. Garnish with cranberries and chives; drizzle with sour cream. 6 servings.

Crème Flan with Fresh Berries

1 pkg. unflavored gelatin

1 cup milk

2 cups half-and-half

¼ cup sugar

1 teaspoon vanilla, divided

15 fresh mint leaves, cut into chiffonade, divided

1 cup orange juice

2 oz. passion fruit compound**

2 passion fruit

½ cantaloupe, cut into balls

¼ honeydew, cut into balls

1 cup quartered strawberries

1 cup raspberries

½ cup blueberries

6 blackberries

¼ cup finely chopped slivered almonds

¼ cup finely chopped pistachios

6 mint leaves

Sprinkle gelatin over ¼ cup milk; let stand 1 minute. Bring remaining milk and half-and-half to a boil in medium saucepan; stir in sugar, gelatin and ½ teaspoon vanilla. Stir until gelatin is completely dissolved. Add several mint leaves. Cool slightly; remove mint leaves. Spray 6 (2.5 oz.) ramekins with nonstick cooking spray or rub lightly with oil. Pour mixture into ramekins; chill until set.

Combine orange juice, passion fruit compound, remaining vanilla and a little fresh mint. Chill several hours. Strain before using. Cut passion fruit in half; spoon out pulp. Reserve. Unmold flan; place in center of individual serving bowls. Surround with 3 cantaloupe balls, 2 honeydew balls, four strawberry quarters, 2 raspberries, two blueberries and 1 blackberry, cut in half. Pour about 2 tablespoons sauce over flan. Sprinkle with mint chiffonade, almonds and pistachios. Garnish with a little bit of passion fruit pulp and a mint leaf.
6 servings.

**Available at some gourmet and cooking specialty stores

Fresh Adriatic Scampi in a Pinot Grigio Nage with Plum Tomatoes, Grilled Radicchio and Parmesan Crostini

Pinot Grigio Nage

1 tablespoon butter

¼ cup chopped shallots

2 tablespoons minced garlic

3 cups pinot grigio wine

½ cup shrimp stock

¼ cup butter, softened

3 plum tomatoes, cut into halves crosswise

¼ cup basil olive oil or pesto

1 radicchio, cut into 6 wedges

2 tablespoons butter, softened

6 (¾-inch thick) slices French baguette

3 tablespoons grated Parmesan cheese

1 tablespoon olive oil

24 scampi, peeled and deveined

4 plum tomatoes, peeled, seeded and finely diced

½ cup chopped fresh parsley

1 teaspoon chopped fresh oregano

1 teaspoon chopped fresh rosemary

Basil oil

6 sprigs fresh oregano, fried

For Pinot Grigio Nage, melt butter in medium saucepan; add shallots and garlic. Cook over medium heat until softened. Add wine; simmer until wine is reduced by half. Add shrimp stock; continue cooking until sauce thickens slightly. Remove from heat; whisk in butter, a little at a time, until emulsion is formed. Keep warm.

Heat oven to 200 degrees F. Place tomato halves in small baking dish. Brush with basil oil or pesto. Place remaining oil in dish. Bake 25 minutes. Heat grill pan; add radicchio. Drizzle with oil; grill 2 minutes on each side. Season to taste with salt and pepper; keep warm. Heat broiler. Spread butter onto bread for crostini; sprinkle with cheese. Broil until lightly browned. Heat oil in large skillet over high heat; add scampi. Cook until opaque.

Place radicchio on serving plates; place baked tomato half partly standing at base of radicchio. Place 4 scampi in front of radicchio. Add chopped tomatoes to sauce; bring to a boil. Remove from heat; stir in parsley, oregano and rosemary. Spoon onto plates; drizzle with basil oil. Garnish with fried oregano sprigs and crostini.
6 servings.

Ahi Tuna on Grilled Pineapple with Wasabe and Lime Mustard

½ cup fresh pineapple
Lime mustard**
1 tablespoon wasabe powder
Water
3 lemon leaves
12 oz. fresh ahi tuna
2 tablespoons clarified butter*

Peel pineapple half; remove center core. Cut into 6 (½-inch) slices; cut into rounds with canapé cutter. Heat stove top grill or grill pan. Grill pineapple slices until lightly browned. Brush with lime mustard. Chill. Mix wasabe with enough water to form a smooth firm mixture. Divide into 12 parts. Shape each into a small pear. Cut 24 thin strips from lemon leaves. Place 2 on each wasabe pear as stems and leaves.

Cut tuna into 12 (1 oz.) chunks. Sear tuna pieces in clarified butter. Place two pieces of tuna on grilled pineapple slice. Garnish with wasabe pears. Serve cold. Sprinkle with sea salt and lime peel, if desired.
6 servings.

*See Chef's Notes

**Tip: Lime mustard is available at most supermarkets. If unavailable add 1 teaspoon lime juice to 2 tablespoons English mustard.

Glass Noodles with Shrimp and Scallions

Cilantro Purée

2 cups fresh cilantro

¼ cup olive oil

2 cloves garlic

2 tablespoons warm water

16 oz. cellophane noodles (glass noodles)

4 green onions, chopped

¼ cup soy sauce, divided

½ teaspoon grated gingerroot, divided

½ teaspoon chopped garlic, divided

¼ cup vegetable oil

1½ lb. peeled, deveined tiger shrimp

Crushed red pepper, to taste

¼ cup oyster sauce

1 teaspoon shrimp paste

1 teaspoon cornstarch

1 tablespoon water

½ cup chopped cilantro

For Cilantro Purée, combine cilantro, oil and garlic in blender container; blend on high until smooth. Stir in water; strain. Reserve.

Soak noodles in hot water until softened; drain.

Combine green onions, 2 tablespoons soy sauce, ¼ teaspoon gingerroot and ¼ teaspoon garlic in small bowl; let stand 15 minutes.

Heat 2 tablespoons oil in wok; add shrimp and crushed red peppers. Stir-fry until shrimp is pink; remove. Keep warm. Add remaining oil to wok (if needed); add Cilantro Purée, remaining gingerroot, remaining garlic, remaining soy sauce, oyster sauce and shrimp paste. Stir-fry briefly. Add shrimp and green onion mixture. Combine cornstarch and water; stir into wok. Cook until thickened. Add drained cellophane noodles; stir-fry briefly. Season with salt and pepper. Add chopped cilantro; toss to combine. 6 servings.

Gravlaks with
Sweet Mustard Dill Sauce

2 lb. fresh salmon fillet with skin
½ cup kosher salt
½ cup sugar
¼ cup chopped fresh dill
1 teaspoon coriander seeds
1 teaspoon cracked mustard seeds
1 teaspoon pepper
1 teaspoon Dijon mustard
2 crushed bay leaves

Sweet Mustard Dill Sauce

¼ cup Dijon mustard
1 tablespoon honey
2 drops lemon juice
1 tablespoon vegetable oil
1 teaspoon chopped fresh dill

¼ cup Dijon mustard
¼ cup chopped fresh dill

Wash salmon. Make small slanted cuts on skin so flesh under the skin gets pickled. Do not make too many cuts as this will damage the flesh. Combine salt, sugar, dill, coriander seeds, mustard seeds, pepper, mustard and bay leaves in small bowl. Spread evenly over salmon; wrap tightly with plastic wrap. Place wrapped salmon in flat dish; cover with weight. Refrigerate 2 days.

For Sweet Mustard Dill Sauce, combine mustard, honey, lemon juice and salt and pepper to taste in small bowl. Whisk in oil until absorbed. Stir in dill.

Remove pickling mixture from salmon. Remove skin. Spread top with mustard; sprinkle with dill. Slice salmon thinly for serving. Serve with Sweet Mustard Dill Sauce. 6 servings.

Soups & Salads

Explore these triumphant pairings of intriguing tastes and textures which showcase gourmet dining at its best and brightest.

Sliced Fennel in a Rich Orange Dressing

Sliced Fennel in a Rich Orange Dressing

4 fennel bulbs

4 oranges

3 tablespoons orange juice concentrate

2 tablespoons Grand Marnier liqueur

2 heads radicchio, separated into leaves

Clean fennel; separate leaves from heart. Coarsely chop half of leaves; reserve remaining leaves for garnish. Slice fennel into thin strips; chill in ice water. Peel oranges; cut into segments over bowl catching juice. Chill orange segments until serving. Combine orange juice concentrate, Grand Marnier and orange juice in medium bowl; mix well. Add chopped fennel leaves; toss to coat. Drain fennel strips; add to bowl. Toss to coat. Cover; refrigerate at least 3 hours.

Arrange radicchio leaves on serving plates; top with salad. Garnish with orange segments and reserved fennel leaves. 6 servings.

Neptune's Chef Salad

1/2 cup chopped red pepper

1/2 cup chopped green pepper

1/4 cup olive oil

1 teaspoon lemon juice

6 (2 oz.) salmon fillets

6 wedges iceberg lettuce

1 lb. Dungeness crabmeat

12 poached ocean scallops

12 oz. peeled cooked shrimp

3 tomatoes, cut into wedges

1 bunch watercress

Combine red pepper, green pepper, oil and lemon juice in food storage bag. Add salmon; toss to coat. Refrigerate 3 to 4 hours. Heat grill or grill pan. Cook salmon until just cooked through. Season with salt and pepper.

Place lettuce on serving plates. Add salmon, crabmeat, scallops and shrimp. Garnish with tomato wedges and watercress. Serve with desired dressing. 6 servings.

White Asparagus and Grilled Scallops in Lobster Vinaigrette

2 raw lobster heads (raw shrimp heads can be used)

6 tablespoons olive oil, divided

½ cup chopped carrot

½ cup chopped onion

¼ cup chopped celery

1 teaspoon tomato paste

1 teaspoon minced garlic

Black peppercorns

¼ cup white wine vinegar

2 lb. ocean scallops

1 can white asparagus, drained

½ leek, cut into strips and steamed

Heat oven to 400 degrees F. Place lobster heads on baking pan; roast until browned, about 40 minutes. Heat 1 tablespoon oil in medium skillet; add carrot, onion and celery. Cook until softened. Stir in tomato paste, garlic and peppercorns. Add lobster heads and 3 tablespoons oil. Reduce heat to low; simmer 30 minutes. Strain; cool. Blend lobster oil with vinegar. Season with salt and pepper.

Heat remaining 1 tablespoon oil in large skillet; add scallops. Cook until firm and cooked through. Season with salt and pepper. Combine scallops and ¾ lobster vinaigrette; chill. Cut asparagus spears in half; add remaining vinaigrette. Chill. Divide asparagus onto serving plates; top with scallops. Garnish with strips of leek. 6 servings.

Spinach, Portobello, Bacon and Blue Cheese in Walnut Dressing

½ cup chopped walnuts

1 teaspoon powdered sugar

¾ cup olive oil

¼ cup vegetable stock*

¼ cup red wine vinegar

1 teaspoon minced garlic

1 teaspoon minced shallots

4 cups fresh baby spinach leaves

2 cups sliced portobello mushrooms

6 slices bacon, cooked and crumbled

½ cup crumbled blue cheese

Heat oven to 375 degrees F. Toss ¼ cup walnuts with about 1 teaspoon powdered sugar. Place on baking sheet. Bake 6 to 8 minutes, stirring occasionally. Watch carefully to avoid burning. Whisk together remaining walnuts, oil, stock, vinegar, garlic and shallots to form dressing. Season with salt and pepper. Combine spinach, mushrooms and bacon in large bowl; add dressing. Toss to coat. Divide onto serving plates. Sprinkle with toasted walnuts and blue cheese.

6 servings.

*See Chef's Notes

Green Bean and Tomato Salad with Goujons of Roasted Lamb Leg

20 cloves garlic, divided

2 lb. leg of lamb

1 sprig rosemary, chopped

2 tablespoons olive oil

1 tablespoon red wine vinegar

1 teaspoon stone ground mustard

1 lb. green beans, cut into 2-inch lengths

3 tomatoes, cubed

½ cup herb vinaigrette*

¼ cup chopped onion

1 teaspoon sugar

½ cup red wine, divided

2 teaspoons tomato paste, divided

1 cup chopped shallots

Thinly slice 5 cloves garlic. Cut small slits into lamb; insert garlic slices. Cover; refrigerate overnight. Heat oven to 375 degrees F. Place lamb in roasting pan; roast until thermometer inserted into thickest part of leg reads 130 degrees F. Cut lamb into strips (goujons). Combine rosemary, olive oil, vinegar and mustard; mix well. Rub onto lamb; marinate 1 hour.

Cook green beans in boiling water 8 to 10 minutes or until tender crisp; drain. Cool in ice water. Combine green beans, tomatoes, vinaigrette, chopped onions and salt and pepper.

Melt sugar in medium heavy skillet; stir in ¼ cup wine and 1 teaspoon tomato paste. Bring mixture to a boil; add shallots. Simmer until sauce is reduced and coats shallots. Chop remaining 15 cloves garlic. Repeat previous steps, using remaining wine and tomato paste.

Divide bean and tomato salad onto serving plates; top with lamb. Garnish with shallots and garlic. Drizzle with remaining vinaigrette. 6 servings.

*See Chef's Notes

Artichokes, Vine Ripened Tomatoes, Fennel and Celery

2 cups julienned fennel

2 cups julienned celery

1 cup creamy Italian dressing, divided

6 canned artichoke hearts, cut into quarters

1 head chicory, separated into leaves

3 tomatoes, peeled, seeded and julienned

2 tablespoons chopped parsley

Combine fennel and celery and ¾ cup dressing in medium bowl; toss to coat. Toss remaining dressing with artichokes. Arrange chicory on serving plates; place fennel and celery salad in center. Garnish with artichokes and tomatoes; sprinkle with parsley. 6 servings.

Chilled Cream of Kir Royal

3 cups vanilla ice cream

1 cup sparkling wine

1 cup whipping cream

¼ cup crème de cassis liqueur

½ teaspoon finely grated gingerroot

1 cup fresh red currants

6 sprigs fresh mint

Place ice cream, wine, cream, liqueur and gingerroot in blender container. Blend on high until smooth. Garnish with currants and mint. Serve immediately. 6 servings.

French Onion Soup

2 tablespoons margarine
6 cups sliced onion
½ teaspoon minced garlic
1 bay leaf
1 cup white wine
6 cups beef stock*
1 sprig fresh thyme
6 thick slices French bread,
cut into rounds
1 cup shredded Swiss
cheese
1 cup shredded Parmesan
cheese

Heat margarine in large skillet; add onions, garlic and bay leaf. Cook over low heat, stirring occasionally, until onions are golden brown, about 45 minutes. Add ½ cup wine; cook until wine is evaporated stirring to loosen browned bits. Add remaining wine, stock and thyme. Season with salt and pepper. Bring mixture to a boil. Reduce heat to low; simmer until onions are very tender, about 1 hour. Remove bay leaf and thyme sprig.

Heat oven to 200 degrees F. Bake bread rounds until dry. Increase oven to 400 degrees F. Mix Swiss and Parmesan cheeses. Place equal amounts of onions in ovenproof soup bowls; fill bowls with soup. Place bread slice in each bowl; sprinkle with cheese mixture. Bake until cheese is golden brown and soup is hot, about 20 minutes. 6 servings.

*See Chef's Notes

Caribbean Pepper Pot

2 tablespoons vegetable oil

1 cup chopped onion

1 teaspoon minced garlic

3 cups sliced okra

1 cup chopped red pepper

1 cup chopped green pepper

1 cup diced potatoes

1 cup diced yams

1 cup quartered and sliced plantain

6 cups chicken stock*

1 cup unsweetened coconut milk

Spaetzle

½ lb. flour

½ cup water

1 egg

1½ teaspoons chopped fresh parsley

2 tablespoons chopped cilantro

Heat oil in Dutch oven; add onions and garlic. Cook until tender. Add okra, red and green peppers, potatoes, yams and plantain. Sauté until lightly browned. Add stock and coconut milk; bring to a boil. Reduce heat to low; simmer 2 to 3 hours or until soup thickens. Season with salt and pepper.

Meanwhile, for Spaetzle, combine flour, water, egg and parsley to form a smooth dough. Bring a large pot of water to a boil. Pass dough through a spaetzle mill or colander with large holes. Cook about 3 minutes or until cooked through. Drain; rinse with cold water.

Add Spaetzle to soup. Garnish with cilantro. 6 servings.

*See Chef's Notes

Chilled Curried Apple Soup

1 tablespoon vegetable oil

¼ cup chopped onion

¼ cup celery

¼ teaspoon minced garlic

3 apples, peeled, cored and diced

1 teaspoon curry powder

¼ teaspoon turmeric

8 cups chicken stock*

1 teaspoon chopped cilantro

¼ cup whipping cream

1 cup chopped apple

Heat olive oil in medium saucepan; add onion, celery and garlic. Cook until softened. Add apples; cook until fork tender. Stir in curry powder and turmeric. Add chicken stock. Bring mixture to a boil. Reduce heat to low; simmer until reduced by half. Add cilantro; cool. Purée in blender or food processor; strain. Stir in cream; season with salt and pepper. Chill several hours. Garnish each serving with chopped apple. 6 servings.

*See Chef's Notes

Game Consommé

5 lb. venison bones

1 gallon water

½ cup chopped carrots

½ cup chopped leeks

½ cup chopped celery

3 egg whites

Black peppercorns, crushed

3 juniper berries

1 bay leaf

¼ cup dry sherry

Heat oven to 400 degrees F. Remove pieces of meat from bones; reserve. Place bones in large roasting pan. Bake 1 hour or until bones are well browned. Add water to bones; stir to remove any browned bits from pan. Simmer 10 minutes. Place bones and water in 6-quart stock pot. Bring mixture to a boil over high heat. Reduce heat to medium; simmer 4 to 5 hours. Strain stock; chill. (There should be about 2 quarts stock.)

Place meat scraps from bones in food processor bowl; process until meat is finely chopped. Combine meat, vegetables, egg whites, peppercorns, juniper berries and bay leaf. Stir meat mixture into cold stock in 4-quart saucepan. Bring mixture to a boil. Reduce heat to low; simmer 2 hours. Strain carefully. Remove any fat. Stir in sherry; season with salt and pepper. 6 servings.

Cream of Red Bliss Potatoes with Chanterelles and Chives

2 tablespoons vegetable oil

¼ cup chopped onion

¼ cup chopped celery

¼ cup chopped leek

½ teaspoon minced garlic

1 sprig fresh thyme

1 sprig fresh marjoram

1 bay leaf

1 lb. red bliss potatoes, diced

6 cups chicken stock*

4 tablespoons butter, divided

1 cup fresh chanterelles**, washed and patted dry

1 cup whipping cream

Chopped fresh chives

Heat oil in large saucepan; add onion, celery, leek, garlic, thyme, marjoram and bay leaf. Cook until vegetables are tender. Stir in potatoes and stock. Bring mixture to a boil. Reduce heat to low; simmer until potatoes are tender. Remove bay leaf. Place soup in blender; blend until smooth. Return to pan. Heat 2 tablespoons butter in small skillet; add mushrooms. Cook until tender; add to soup. Stir in cream and remaining butter. Season to taste with salt and pepper. Sprinkle each serving with chives.
6 servings.

*See Chef's Notes

**Tip: Dried chanterelles can be used. Rehydrate in hot water before using.

Cream of Green Asparagus with Tomato Confetti

Tomato Confetti

1 tablespoon olive oil

½ teaspoon minced garlic

2 tomatoes, peeled, seeded and diced

½ bunch fresh basil leaves

1 teaspoon sugar

Asparagus Soup

1 lb. asparagus

4 cups chicken stock*

1 teaspoon roux*

2 cups milk

½ cup half-and-half

Grated nutmeg

½ cup whipping cream

For Tomato Confetti, heat olive oil in medium skillet; add garlic. Cook until tender; stir in tomatoes, basil and sugar. Cook until heated through; keep warm.

For Asparagus Soup, rinse asparagus; snap off stalk ends. Break off tips; reserve. Dice asparagus stalks. Bring stock to a boil in large saucepan; stir in roux. Reduce heat to low; simmer 30 minutes or until thickened, stirring occasionally. Cook asparagus tips in boiling water 3 to 4 minutes until tender crisp. Remove; set aside. Cook diced asparagus in boiling water 2 to 3 minutes, until tender crisp. Drain; place in blender container. Blend until puréed. Stir into stock. Add milk, half-and-half and nutmeg to taste. Simmer 15 minutes. Stir in cream and asparagus tips. Season with salt and pepper. Spoon soup into serving cups and top with tomatoes. 6 servings.

*See Chef's Notes

Lobster Bisque

1 (2 lb.) lobster

6½ tablespoons butter, divided

½ teaspoon minced garlic

½ cup chopped celery

½ cup chopped carrots

½ cup chopped onion

¼ cup tomato paste

6 cups fish stock*

1 tablespoon brandy

1½ tablespoons flour

1 cup whipping cream

¼ cup sherry

Remove lobster meat from shell; chop. Refrigerate until needed. Coarsely chop shell. Heat 3 tablespoons butter in medium stock pot; add shell and garlic. Cook until browned. Add celery, carrots and onion; cook until softened. Add tomato paste; cook 5 minutes, stirring constantly. Add fish stock and brandy; bring to a boil. Reduce heat to low; simmer 1 hour, stirring occasionally. Meanwhile, heat 1½ tablespoons butter in small saucepan over low heat; add flour. Cook 20 minutes, stirring constantly, until deep golden brown. Stir into soup. Continue simmering 45 minutes longer, stirring often. Strain; return to stock pot. Stir in cream and sherry. Heat remaining butter in small skillet; add lobster. Cook until opaque; add to soup. 6 servings.

*See Chef's Notes

Pasta

Our journey now takes us to the shores of Italy, where we celebrate deliciously authentic pastas rich with mushrooms, basil, garlic and Parmesan.

Ziti with Italian Sausage, Bell Peppers and Mushroom Tomato Sauce

Ziti with Italian Sausage, Bell Peppers and Mushroom Tomato Sauce

1½ lb. ziti

2 lb. bulk Italian sausage

¼ cup olive oil

1 cup sliced mushrooms

1 tablespoon minced fresh garlic

3 cups tomato sauce*

2 green peppers, roasted, peeled and chopped

2 red peppers, roasted, peeled and chopped

½ cup chopped ripe olives

½ cup shredded Parmesan cheese

1 tablespoon chopped fresh parsley

Cook ziti according to package directions; drain. Keep warm. Cook sausage in large skillet over medium heat until lightly browned; drain fat. Heat olive oil in medium skillet; add mushrooms and garlic. Cook until tender. Combine sausage, mushrooms, tomato sauce and roasted green and red peppers. Cook over medium heat until heated through; toss with pasta. Divide onto serving plates. Sprinkle with olives, cheese and parsley. 6 servings.

*See Chef's Notes

Homemade Potato Gnocchi with Truffles

Potato Gnocchi

4 (about 6 oz. each) baking potatoes

1½ cups all-purpose flour

¾ cup grated Parmesan cheese

2 eggs, beaten

½ teaspoon salt

Grated nutmeg

4 tablespoons truffle butter

1 black truffle**

For Potato Gnocchi; bake potatoes in 400 degree F. oven until tender when pierced with a fork (about 40 to 50 minutes). Cool slightly; peel. Press through a ricer. Combine potatoes, flour, cheese, eggs, salt, pepper and nutmeg in medium bowl. Mix well to form a soft dough. Divide into quarters. Roll each quarter into ½-inch thick rope. Cut into 1-inch pieces. Roll off tines of a fork to form characteristic shape.

Bring large pot of salted water to a boil; add Potato Gnocchi. Boil until cooked through, about 6 minutes; drain. Toss gnocchi with truffle butter. Divide into serving bowls; shave black truffle over each. Serve immediately. 6 servings.

**Tip: Use porcini, chanterelles or other wild mushrooms in place of black truffle.

Hay and Straw

½ cup sun-dried tomatoes

1 lb. fresh spinach fettuccine

1 lb. fresh egg fettuccine

¼ cup olive oil

1 teaspoon minced garlic

4 cups tomato sauce*

2 tablespoons chopped fresh basil

Parmesan cheese

Place sun-dried tomatoes in small bowl; cover with hot water. When softened, drain and cut into thin slices. Cook spinach fettuccine and egg fettuccine in separate pots of boiling water. Drain; keep warm. Heat olive oil in medium skillet; add garlic and drained sun-dried tomatoes. Cook until garlic is tender. Add tomato sauce and basil; cook until heated through. Season with salt and pepper. Toss pasta with sauce. Divide pasta onto serving plates; sprinkle with cheese. 6 servings.

*See Chef's Notes

Saffron Pappardelle with Grilled Shiitake Mushrooms and Sun-dried Tomatoes

1 cup sun-dried tomatoes

1 cup whipping cream

Pinch saffron

2 cups hot chicken veloute sauce

1½ lb. pappardelle

1 tablespoon olive oil

2 cups quartered shiitake mushrooms

1 teaspoon minced garlic

1 cup grated Parmesan cheese

1 tablespoon chopped fresh basil

1 tablespoon chopped fresh parsley

Place sun-dried tomatoes in small bowl; cover with hot water. When softened, drain and cut into thin slices. Combine cream and saffron in small saucepan. Bring to a boil; reduce heat to low. Simmer until reduced by half; strain. Add to veloute sauce; keep warm. Cook pappardelle according to package directions; drain. Keep warm. Meanwhile, heat oil in medium skillet; add mushrooms, garlic and sun-dried tomatoes. Sauté over high heat about 5 minutes or until mushrooms are cooked. Season with salt and pepper. Combine pasta and sauce; toss to coat. Sprinkle with mushroom mixture, Parmesan cheese, basil and parsley. 6 servings.

Fusilli Tossed in a Roma Tomato Sauce with Tuna Chunks

6 cups fusilli

2 tablespoons olive oil

½ teaspoon minced garlic

2 (6 oz.) cans chunk light tuna in water, drained and chunked

3 cups chunky tomato sauce*

Cook fusilli according to package directions. Drain; keep warm. Heat olive oil in medium saucepan; add garlic. Cook until garlic is tender; add tuna. Cook until tuna is heated through. Stir in tomato sauce. Cook until heated through. Season with salt and pepper. Combine pasta and sauce in large bowl; toss to coat. 6 servings.

*See Chef's Notes

Fettuccine with Mushroom Sauce and Chicken Tenders

Chicken Veloute

2 cups chicken stock*

1 1/2 tablespoons roux*

4 oz. dried porcini mushrooms

2 lb. chicken tenderloins

1/2 cup olive oil

1 teaspoon minced garlic

2 sprigs fresh thyme, chopped

1 tablespoon clarified butter*

1/4 cup chopped onion

2 cups sliced mushrooms

1 cup whipping cream

1 1/2 lb. fresh fettuccine

1/4 cup chopped fresh parsley

For Chicken Veloute, bring stock to a boil in medium saucepan; reduce heat to low. Whisk in roux; simmer 30 to 40 minutes or until thickened. Soak porcini in hot water for 20 minutes. Drain well; chop.

Combine tenderloins, olive oil, garlic and thyme in food storage bag; toss to coat chicken. Marinate at least 30 minutes. Season with salt and pepper. Heat butter in medium skillet; add onions. Cook until onions are golden. Add mushrooms and porcini; simmer 5 minutes. Add chicken veloute; bring mixture to a boil. Season with salt and pepper. Remove from heat; add cream. Keep warm.

Cook pasta to desired doneness in boiling salted water; drain. Toss with mushroom sauce; keep warm. Heat large skillet until hot; add chicken. Cook over medium-high heat until no longer pink. Season with salt and pepper. Divide pasta onto serving plates; top with chicken. Sprinkle with chopped parsley. 6 servings.

*See Chef's Notes

Cappellini in Olive Oil and Basil

1 cup virgin olive oil, divided

1 tablespoon minced garlic

2 lb. fresh cappellini

½ cup baby capers, drained

1 cup fresh basil, finely chopped

1 cup Parmesan cheese

Heat 2 tablespoons olive oil in small skillet; add garlic. Cook until garlic is tender. Cook cappellini in salted boiling water 2 to 3 minutes or until "al dente." Pasta should retain a little firmness. Drain. Toss with remaining ingredients. Season with salt and freshly ground pepper. 6 servings.

Linguini al Genovese

2 cups fresh basil, finely chopped

½ cup pine nuts

½ cup Parmesan cheese

½ cup Pecorino cheese

1 tablespoon minced garlic

1 cup virgin olive oil

2 lb. fresh linguini

Combine basil, pine nuts, Parmesan cheese, Pecorino cheese and garlic in blender container; blend until coarsely chopped. Slowly add oil with motor running; blend until thick sauce forms. Cook linguini in boiling salted water 4 to 8 minutes or until "al dente". Pasta should retain a little firmness. Drain. Combine pasta and sauce in large bowl; toss to coat. 6 servings

Entrées

We arrive at the heart of the meal. Full of international flair, these dishes bring you a whole new world of exotic flavors and sensational presentations.

Broiled Alaskan King Crab Legs with Bitter Lemon Butter

Broiled Alaskan King Crab Legs with Bitter Lemon Butter

Crab Consommé

2 cups water

6 crab bodies

2 lobster heads

¼ cup chopped celery

¼ cup chopped leek

¼ cup chopped onion

5 oz. fish trimmings

1 tomato, chopped

1 egg white

½ teaspoon tomato paste

5 black peppercorns

Bitter Lemon Butter

2 lemons

1 lime

1 grapefruit

1 cup butter

1 teaspoon sugar

¼ teaspoon lime juice

4 purple potatoes

2 carrots

1 zucchini

5 lb. king crab legs

¼ cup butter, melted

2 batches watercress

6 slices lime

For Crab Consommé, combine water, crab bodies, lobster heads, celery, leek and onion in small saucepan; bring to a boil. Reduce heat; simmer 20 minutes. Strain and chill. Mince fish trimmings, tomato, egg white, tomato paste and peppercorns together. Add to cold stock. Bring mixture to a boil; reduce heat to very low. Cook about 45 minutes. Strain through cheesecloth.

For Bitter Lemon Butter, cut rind from lemons, lime and grapefruit. Place butter and rinds in small saucepan; bring to a boil. Remove from heat; let stand until layers separate. Pour off milky solids; strain. Cut lime and grapefruit into segments over bowl catching juices. Melt sugar in small saucepan; add lime and grapefruit segments. Cook until caramelized. Remove from heat; squeeze juice from caramelized segments. Stir juice into butter; add lime juice.

Cut potatoes, carrots and zucchini into small balls. Cook in boiling water until tender crisp. Toss with a little lemon butter. Place crab legs on baking sheet; brush with butter. Broil about 6 minutes or until just cooked.

Pour ¼ cup Crab Consommé into serving bowls; arrange crab legs in bowl. Drizzle with lemon butter; add vegetables. Garnish with watercress and lime slices. 6 servings.

Tamarind Rubbed Prime Rib of American Beef

Marinade

1 cup vegetable oil

¼ cup balsamic vinegar

1 tablespoon chopped gingerroot

1 tablespoon tamarind pulp**

2 tablespoons honey

1 teaspoon crushed red pepper

1 teaspoon ground cumin

1 tablespoon chopped cilantro

8 lb. prime rib roast

Baked potatoes

Grilled leeks

Combine Marinade ingredients except cilantro in small saucepan; bring to a boil. Remove from heat; stir in cilantro.

Rub Marinade all over roast. Cover; refrigerate no longer than 6 hours. Heat oven to 300 degrees F. Remove roast from marinade. Roast about 3 hours or until desired doneness (150 degrees F. for medium). Let roast stand at least 20 minutes before slicing. Serve with baked potato and grilled leeks. 6 servings.

**Tip: Tamarind pulp can be found in some Middle Eastern and East Indian grocery stores.

Jerked Pork Loin

1 cup finely chopped carrot

1 cup finely chopped celery

1 cup finely chopped onion

½ cup vegetable oil

3 green onions, finely chopped

1 tablespoon minced garlic

1 tablespoon soy sauce

2 teaspoons jerk seasoning

1 teaspoon crushed red pepper flakes

½ teaspoon ground cumin

3 lb. boneless center-cut pork loin roast

Combine ingredients except pork; mix well. Place pork in container with cover; add marinade. Rub into meat. Cover; refrigerate 24 hours. Remove from marinade; pat dry. Heat oven to 350 degrees F. Place pork in roasting pan. Roast about 1 hour until meat thermometer reaches 160 degrees F. Let roast stand 20 minutes before slicing. 6 servings.

Oven Fresh Focaccia with Arugula, Mozzarella, Tomatoes and Roasted Red Bell Peppers

Basil Vinaigrette

¼ cup olive oil

1 teaspoon balsamic vinegar

1 teaspoon red wine vinegar

1 teaspoon chopped fresh basil

2 shallots, chopped

2 cloves garlic, minced

¼ cup olive oil

2 tablespoons balsamic vinegar

4 cloves garlic, minced

6 individual focaccia rolls**

2 roasted red bell peppers, cut into squares

2 roasted green bell peppers, cut into squares

1 tablespoon mayonnaise

1 cup pesto

3 bunches arugula, washed, torn

1 lb. fresh mozzarella cheese, sliced

3 beefsteak tomatoes, sliced

Italian-style pickled vegetables

Combine all ingredients for Basil Vinaigrette; mix well. Chill.

Heat oven to 250 degrees F. Combine oil, balsamic vinegar and garlic in small bowl; brush all over focaccia. Bake until crisp. Meanwhile, add roasted red and green peppers to olive oil mixture. Let stand until needed. Cut focaccia crosswise into halves; brush both cut sides with mayonnaise and pesto. Arrange arugula, red peppers, mozzarella, green peppers and sliced tomatoes alternately in two layers on bottom of bread. Drizzle with Basil Vinaigrette. Add top of bread. Garnish with Italian-style pickled vegetables. 6 servings.

**Tip: One large loaf of focaccia cut into 6 wedges may be used if individual rolls are unavailable.

Chinese Pepper Steak

Marinade

1 tablespoon chopped gingerroot

1 tablespoon minced garlic

2 tablespoons soy sauce

1 tablespoon sesame oil

2 lb. beef tenderloin, cut into strips ¼ inch wide

¼ cup sesame oil

2 tablespoons vegetable oil

1 red pepper, cut into diamonds

1 green pepper, cut into diamonds

1 cup diagonally sliced carrots

1 cup coarsely chopped onion (¾ inch pieces)

1 cup snow pea pods

1 tablespoon minced garlic

1 tablespoon gingerroot

½ cup soy sauce

2 tablespoons oyster sauce

1 tablespoon cornstarch

3 tablespoons water

1 small can baby corn, drained, cut in halves

1 small can sliced bamboo shoots, drained

2 tablespoons toasted sesame seed

Chopped green onions

Combine Marinade ingredients except beef; mix well. Place beef in container with cover; add Marinade. Toss to coat. Cover; refrigerate 6 hours. Remove from marinade; pat dry.

Heat sesame oil and oil in wok until hot; add beef. Stir-fry until browned. Remove; keep warm. Add peppers; stir-fry until softened but still crisp. Remove; keep warm. Repeat with carrots, onion and pea pods. When vegetables are cooked add garlic and gingerroot to wok. Stir-fry until tender; stir in soy sauce and oyster sauce. Combine cornstarch and water; stir into wok. Cook until thickened. Add beef, vegetables, baby corn and bamboo shoots; cook until heated through. Sprinkle with sesame seed and green onions before serving. 6 servings.

East Indian Chicken Curry

1 tablespoon curry powder

1 tablespoon minced gingerroot

1 tablespoon minced garlic

1 teaspoon turmeric

6 boneless skinless split chicken breasts, cubed

3 tablespoons vegetable oil

2 cups sliced red onion

2 large tomatoes, peeled, seeded, and chopped

1 tablespoon chopped cilantro

1 teaspoon cumin seed

1 teaspoon coriander seeds

3 cardamom pods

3 whole cloves

1 cinnamon stick

3 chopped dried red chiles

2 cups unsweetened coconut milk

Raita

1 cup plain yogurt

2 tablespoons chopped red onion

2 tablespoons chopped cucumber

2 tablespoons chopped tomato

1 tablespoon lime juice

1 teaspoon ground cumin

Rice

Fried papadums

Combine curry, gingerroot, garlic and turmeric in small bowl; add chicken. Toss to coat; place in food storage bag. Refrigerate 1 hour or longer. Heat oil in medium skillet; add onions, tomatoes, cilantro, cumin seed, coriander, cardamom, cloves, cinnamon and red chiles. Cook over medium heat until very soft and oil separates. Add chicken; cook 5 minutes or until lightly browned. Add coconut milk; reduce heat to low. Simmer 20 minutes or until sauce thickens. Remove cloves and cinnamon stick.

Meanwhile combine all ingredients for Raita. Refrigerate until serving.

Serve curry with rice, Raita and fried papadums. 6 servings.

Medallion of Ostrich with Foie Gras

3 lb. ostrich fan fillet

3 cups red wine

1 cup chopped onion

1 apple, coarsely chopped

2 cloves garlic, minced

1 teaspoon white peppercorns

1 teaspoon juniper berries

1 bay leaf

½ lb. baking potatoes, peeled and cut into 1-inch cubes

½ lb. celery root, peeled and cut into 1-inch cubes

2 cups whipping cream

4 tablespoons butter, divided

2 cups chicken glaze*

¼ teaspoon crushed juniper berries

½ lb. Brussels sprouts, ends trimmed and leaves separated

1 lb. carrots, cut into small balls

Olive oil

1 lb. foie gras

Fresh raspberries

¼ lb. bacon, cooked, crumbled

Trim the fan fillet; remove membrane. Cut into 6 (7 oz.) steaks. Place steaks in container with cover. Add wine, onion, apple, garlic, peppercorns, juniper berries and bay leaf; mix to coat meat. Seal container. Refrigerate 48 hours.

In medium saucepan, cook potatoes and celery root in boiling water 8 to 10 minutes; drain. Add cream; reduce heat to low. Simmer until tender, stirring occasionally. Season with salt; add 2 tablespoons butter. Mash; keep warm.

In medium saucepan, combine chicken glaze and crushed juniper berries. Cook until slightly thickened; strain. Whisk in 1 tablespoon butter. Keep warm. In medium saucepan, cook Brussels sprouts leaves briefly in boiling water; drain. Chill in ice water. Cook carrots in boiling water until tender; drain. Melt 1 tablespoon butter in medium skillet; add sprout leaves. Cook until lightly browned; add carrots. Cook until heated through, season with salt and pepper. Keep warm.

Heat oven to 375 degrees F. Remove ostrich from marinade. Heat olive oil in large ovenproof skillet; add ostrich. Cook over high heat until browned, sealing in juices. Bake about 6 minutes for medium doneness. Peel fine skin off foie gras; cut into ½-inch slices. Heat skillet to very hot; cook foie gras briefly to seal in juices. Season with salt and pepper.

Place mashed potato-celery root mixture onto serving plates; add ostrich steak. Top with foie gras. Garnish with Brussels sprouts and carrots. Add raspberries. Drizzle with chicken glaze and top with crumbled bacon. 6 servings.

*See Chef's Notes

Soft Shell Crabs with Drawn Butter

Saffron Rice

1 tablespoon butter

1 tablespoon chopped onion

2 cups white rice

4 cups water

1 teaspoon salt

1 pinch saffron

½ cup cooked peas

Parsley Emulsion

1 cup Italian parsley

2 tablespoons olive oil

¼ teaspoon minced garlic

¼ teaspoon lemon juice

Drawn Butter

½ cup butter

1 teaspoon grated lemon rind

2 cloves garlic

Vegetable oil for frying

1 cup all-purpose flour

3 eggs

Water

1 tablespoon chopped cilantro

1 teaspoon lemon juice

1 teaspoon ginger juice (from grated gingerroot)

12 (3 oz.) soft shell crabs

For Saffron Rice, heat butter in medium saucepan; add onion. Cook until onion is softened; stir in rice. Cook until rice is coated with butter. Add water, salt and saffron. Bring to a boil; cover. Reduce heat to low; simmer until water is absorbed, about 15 minutes. Stir in peas; keep warm.

For Parsley Emulsion, cook parsley in boiling water 1 minute or until color brightens. Drain; chill in ice water. Drain; purée using hand held blender. Strain through cheesecloth, saving juice. Slowly whisk oil, garlic and lemon juice into parsley juice forming an emulsion. Season with salt and pepper.

For Drawn Butter, heat butter, lemon rind and garlic in small saucepan. Bring to a simmer. Remove from heat; let stand until milk solids separate. Pour off fat; strain.

Heat about ½ inch oil in large deep skillet. Combine flour and eggs in medium bowl; add water until batter is formed. (It must be thick enough to coat.) Add cilantro, lemon juice and ginger juice. Season with salt. Dip crabs into batter; add to skillet. Fry until golden brown and cooked through.

Serve crabs with Saffron Rice and Drawn Butter. Drizzle with Parsley Emulsion.
6 servings.

Grilled Chateaubriand

3 lb. beef tenderloin, cut from center
1 tablespoon Dijon mustard
Bearnaise sauce
Broccoli spears
Mashed potatoes

Heat oven to 375 degrees F. Season meat with salt and pepper. Heat grill pan until very hot; add meat. Cook over high heat until browned on all sides sealing in juices. Place in roasting pan; spread with mustard. Roast 20 minutes for medium rare (150 degrees F.). Let rest 10 minutes before slicing. Serve with Bearnaise sauce, broccoli spears and mashed potatoes. 6 servings.

Glazed Rack of Veal with Morels, Calvados Jus and Rosemary Emulsion

12 fresh morels
2 cups warm veal stock
1 teaspoon minced garlic
3 sprigs rosemary, chopped
1 rack of veal (6 ribs), chine bone removed
½ cup Calvados (apple brandy)
2 cups white wine
1 cup demi-glace*
¼ cup apple juice
¼ cup butter
¼ cup chopped shallots
Rosemary emulsion

Clean morels; add to veal stock. Remove when softened; reserve stock. Heat oven to 350 degrees F. Combine garlic and rosemary; rub over veal. Season with salt and pepper. Place in roasting pan. Roast about 1½ hours until veal is medium doneness (160 degrees F.). Baste occasionally with veal stock. Remove veal; keep warm. Add Calvados. When heated carefully ignite with long match. Add wine; cook until reduced. Add demi-glace and apple juice; simmer until liquid measures about 1½ cups. Strain; season with salt and pepper. Heat butter in medium skillet; add shallots. Cook until soft; add morels. Cook briefly. Add a little Calvados jus and simmer 1 minute. Slice veal into ribs; place on serving plates. Top each with 2 morels. Drizzle with Calvados jus and rosemary emulsion. 6 servings.

*See Chef's Notes

Broiled Lobster Tail with Melted Butter

Mushroom Risotto

1 tablespoon butter

1 tablespoon chopped onion

¼ teaspoon minced garlic

2 cups sliced mushrooms

1½ cups Arborio rice

2 tablespoons white wine

1 bay leaf

3 cups hot chicken stock*

¼ cup Parmesan cheese

1 teaspoon chopped fresh parsley

6 lobster tails

1 cup butter, melted

For Mushroom Risotto, heat butter in medium saucepan; add onion and garlic. Cook over medium high heat until softened. Add mushrooms; cook until lightly browned. Stir in rice. Add wine; cook 1 minute. Reduce heat to low. Add bay leaf; stir in 1 cup stock. Continue stirring until stock is absorbed. Continue adding stock ½ cup at a time and stirring until absorbed; remove bay leaf. Remove from heat; stir in cheese and parsley.

Heat broiler. Cut the top of the lobster tail and pull meat over shell without loosening it from the shell. Dip in butter; place on baking sheet. Spread tail fins. Bring remaining butter to a boil; let stand until milk solids separate. Pour off clarified butter layer. Broil lobster about 4 inches from heat for 8 minutes or until done. Serve with risotto and clarified butter. 6 servings.

*See Chef's Notes

Grilled Fillet of Fresh Pacific Salmon with Dill Mousseline

Dill Mousseline

½ cup whipping cream

½ cup hollandaise sauce

2 tablespoons chopped fresh dill

2 lb. purple potatoes

Butter

6 (6 oz.) salmon fillets, with skin

2 cups creamed spinach

2 tablespoons vanilla vinaigrette

Dill sprigs

Whip cream on high until soft peaks form; fold in hollandaise. Add dill; mix to blend. Chill.

Cut potatoes into medium balls. Cook in boiling water 5 minutes; drain. Heat butter in medium skillet; add potatoes. Cook until browned and tender; keep warm. Heat grill or grill pan to very hot; oil lightly. Cut slashes in skin of salmon; do not cut fish. Season with salt and pepper. Quickly cook salmon on both sides, skin side first. Place in greased baking pan skin side up. Broil until fish is just cooked through but still moist. Place ⅓ cup creamed spinach in center of serving plates. Arrange salmon, skin side up, over spinach. Add 3 potatoes; drizzle with vinaigrette. Top with Dill Mousseline and garnish with dill sprig. 6 servings.

Chicken Tetrazzini

6 boneless skinless split chicken breasts, each cut into 6 slices

2 tablespoons olive oil

1 lb. fettuccine

4 cups creamy mushroom sauce*

1 cup shredded Cheddar cheese

6 basil leaves

Season chicken with salt and pepper. Heat olive oil in large skillet; add chicken. Cook 3 minutes or until no longer pink in center. Do not overcook. Cook fettuccine according to package directions. Drain; toss with mushroom sauce. Heat broiler. Divide pasta onto ovenproof serving plates; add 6 chicken strips to each. Spoon a little sauce over chicken; sprinkle with cheese. Broil until cheese is melted. Garnish with basil leaves. 6 servings.

*See Chef's Notes

Roast Leg of New Zealand Spring Lamb with Rosemary Reduction

6 cloves garlic

3 lb. leg of lamb

1 cup olive oil

6 sprigs fresh thyme, chopped

3 sprigs fresh rosemary, chopped

1 cup lamb jus

Fresh rosemary

1 tablespoon water

1 teaspoon cornstarch

1/4 cup mint jelly

Cut 4 cloves garlic into slices; chop remaining garlic. Cut small slits into lamb, about 1/2 inch deep. Insert at least 10 slices garlic into lamb. Combine olive oil, remaining garlic, thyme and rosemary. Rub into meat. Place lamb in container with cover. Cover; refrigerate 48 hours. Remove lamb from marinade. Place on roasting rack. Roast to desired doneness, about 1 hour for rare (140 degrees F.) to 1 1/2 hours for well done (170 degrees F.). Combine lamb jus and rosemary; bring mixture to a boil. Reduce heat to low; simmer 15 minutes. Combine water and cornstarch; stir into lamb jus. Continue cooking until slightly thickened. Season with salt and pepper. Slice lamb. Serve with sauce and mint jelly. 6 servings.

Grilled Fillet of Macadamia Nut Crusted Chilean Sea Bass on Chinese Long Life Beans

Thinly sliced peeled gingerroot

Thinly sliced peeled yams

Vegetable oil

½ cup unsweetened coconut milk

2 stalks lemon grass, coarsely chopped

¼ teaspoon hot pepper sauce

1 tablespoon butter

Salsa

2 teaspoons olive oil

2 shallots, chopped

1 teaspoon sugar

1 tablespoon lemon juice

1 teaspoon rice wine vinegar

1 avocado, diced

1 papaya, diced

1 tomato, peeled, seeded, chopped

1 tablespoon pomegranate seeds

1 teaspoon chopped fresh cilantro

6 (7 oz. each) sea bass fillets

½ cup finely chopped macadamia nuts

1 tablespoon vegetable oil

½ teaspoon coriander seeds

½ teaspoon cumin seed

½ teaspoon fennel seed

1 plantain, cut into wedges, blanched

1 yam, peeled, cut into wedges, blanched

2 tablespoons butter

1 lb. Chinese long beans, blanched

Fry gingerroot and sliced yam in hot oil until crisp; set aside. Bring coconut milk and lemon grass to a boil in medium saucepan. Reduce heat to low; simmer 30 minutes. Cool; add hot pepper sauce and season with salt and pepper. Strain; return to heat. Whisk softened butter into warmed sauce. Keep warm.

Heat olive oil in small skillet for Salsa; add shallot. Cook over medium heat until shallot is tender. Remove from heat; cool. Stir together sugar, lemon juice and vinegar in medium bowl. Add sautéed shallot, avocado, papaya, tomato, pomegranate seeds and cilantro; mix gently. Season with salt and pepper.

Heat oven to 350 degrees F. Coat one side of fillets with macadamia nuts. Heat oil in ovenproof large skillet over high heat; add fillets coated side up. Cook until browned on bottom sealing in juices. Place in oven; bake 6 to 8 minutes or until cooked through but still moist.

Toast coriander, cumin and fennel seeds in small skillet; cool. Crush. Meanwhile, sauté plantain and yam wedges in butter until tender. Add toasted seeds; season with salt and pepper. Sauté long beans in remaining butter until tender; season with salt and pepper.

Place yams and plantains in center of individual serving plates; top with long beans. Add fish; drizzle with coconut sauce and Salsa. Sprinkle with fried gingerroot and yams. 6 servings.

Mongolian Steak Salad

1 orange

3 (10 oz.) top sirloin steaks

2 tablespoons soy sauce

1 tablespoon honey

2 teaspoons minced garlic

1 teaspoon chopped gingerroot

Dressing

½ cup sesame oil

1 teaspoon Dijon mustard

½ cup rice wine vinegar

1 tablespoon chopped shallot

1 teaspoon minced garlic

½ teaspoon chopped fresh tarragon

½ head iceberg lettuce, torn into bite-size pieces

½ head romaine lettuce, torn into bite-size pieces

1 cup spinach leaves

1 cup frisee

12 sprigs watercress, tough stems removed

1 head radicchio, torn into bite-size pieces

1 teaspoon toasted sesame seed

6 Belgian endive leaves

6 red pepper sticks

Grate rind from orange; squeeze juice. Place steaks in container with lid. Mix orange juice, orange rind, soy sauce, honey, garlic and gingerroot; pour over steaks. Cover; refrigerate 2 to 3 hours.

For Dressing, using wire whisk, slowly add oil to mustard; whisk until thickened. Add vinegar, shallot, garlic and tarragon. Season with salt and pepper.

Combine iceberg lettuce, romaine, spinach, frisee, watercress and radicchio in large bowl; toss. Add dressing; toss to coat. Divide onto serving plates. Heat grill. Season steaks with salt and pepper. Grill to medium-rare doneness. Slice each steak into 10 slices. Place 5 slices steak on each plate. Sprinkle with sesame seed. Garnish with Belgian endive leaf and red pepper stick. 6 servings.

Japanese Salad

Ponzu Vinaigrette

2 cups mirin

1 cup soy sauce

1 cup rice wine vinegar

¼ cup sunflower oil

1 tablespoon sesame oil

2 teaspoons dried bonito flakes**

2 teaspoons chopped gingerroot

3 green onions, chopped

1 green chile, minced

4 oz. rice noodles (rice sticks)

Vegetable oil for frying

6 oz. soba noodles

2 cups vegetable broth

¼ cup teriyaki sauce

1 cup sliced shiitake mushrooms

18 shrimp, peeled and deveined

1 teaspoon tokarishi seasoning**

4 chicken tenderloins, sliced

1 carrots, peeled and shredded

½ cup sliced bok choy

½ cup chopped green onions

1 cup blanched snow pea pods

½ cup pickled ginger

4 teaspoons black sesame seeds

Combine all ingredients for Ponzu Vinaigrette in container with tight-fitting lid. Shake well to blend. Chill.

Fry the rice noodles in hot oil. They will puff as they cook. Remove; drain. Cook soba noodles in vegetable broth. Drain; chill. Heat teriyaki sauce in medium skillet; add mushrooms. Cook until mushrooms are tender. Chill. Heat grill. Season shrimp with tokarishi; grill. Grill chicken. Toss soba noodles, carrots, bok choy and green onions in 1 cup vinaigrette. Divide into serving bowls. Add shrimp and chicken. Sprinkle with mushrooms. Add rice noodles. Create fans from snow pea pods; stand upright in salads. Form roses from pickled ginger; place on salads. Sprinkle with sesame seeds. 6 servings.

**Available at Asian food stores

Roast Petaluma Capon

¼ cup butter, softened

1 tablespoon minced garlic

1 tablespoon chopped fresh rosemary

1 (6 lb.) capon

5 cups chicken stock, divided*

1 tablespoon butter

½ cup chopped onion

1 teaspoon minced garlic

3 cups diced white bread

2 cups chopped apples

1 teaspoon chopped fresh thyme

½ teaspoon chopped fresh oregano

2 eggs, beaten

2 cups cranberry sauce

Heat oven to 350 degrees F. Combine butter, garlic, rosemary and salt and pepper to taste; rub over capon. Truss; place in roasting pan. Roast until thermometer inserted between thigh and breast registers 175 degrees F., about 2½ hours. Baste occasionally with chicken stock. Remove from oven; let stand 20 minutes.

Meanwhile, heat oven to 375 degrees F. Heat butter in small skillet; add onions and garlic. Cook until onions are tender. Stir in diced white bread and stock; remove from heat. Add apples and herbs; stir in eggs. Place in buttered 8-inch square baking dish. Bake 45 to 55 minutes or until cooked through and browned.

Cut capon into halves. Separate legs and breasts; remove bones. Slice meat. Place scoop of stuffing in center of serving plates; arrange light and dark meat over stuffing. Drizzle with pan juices. Serve with cranberry sauce. 6 servings.

*See Chef's Notes

Salmon Paillard

Lemon Dill Sabayon
2 tablespoons butter
½ cup chopped shallots
½ teaspoon chopped garlic
1 cup white wine
1 cup fish stock*
1 tablespoon lemon juice
½ teaspoon cornstarch
½ teaspoon water
3 egg yolks
2 tablespoons chopped fresh dill

1 cup sliced leeks
1 large carrot, cut into matchsticks
1 lb. zucchini, cut into matchsticks
1 lb. yellow squash, cut into matchsticks
2 lb. purple potatoes, peeled, cut into balls
½ cup butter
3 lb. salmon fillet
½ cup olive oil

Melt butter for sabayon in medium saucepan for Lemon Dill Sabayon; add shallots and garlic. Cook over medium heat until softened. Add wine; cook until liquid is reduced to 1 to 2 tablespoons. Add stock and lemon juice; cook until reduced to about ¾ cup. Mix cornstarch and water; stir into sauce. Bring to a boil; reduce heat and simmer 10 minutes. Remove from heat; cool slightly. Whisk some sauce into egg yolks to warm them; whisk warmed yolks into remaining sauce. Place over double boiler. Cook, whisking constantly, until foamy. Remove from heat. Stir in dill. Season to taste with salt and pepper.

Blanch vegetables in boiling water; cool in ice water. Cook potatoes in boiling water until tender; drain. Heat 2 tablespoons butter in large skillet. Sauté potato balls until lightly browned. Keep warm. Reheat zucchini, squash, leeks and carrots in butter. Keep warm.

Freeze salmon fillets several hours or until slightly frozen. Cut into very thin slices. Heat oil in large skillet. Add salmon slices; do not crowd. Cook, turning once, one minute on each side. Remove from pan; keep warm. Repeat with remaining salmon. Arrange salmon slices in overlapping manner on serving plates. Place potato balls around salmon. Add vegetables. Drizzle with Lemon Dill Sabayon. 6 servings.

*See Chef's Notes

Grilled Paillard of Young Turkey Harlequin

2 turkey drumsticks

2 cups corn kernels

3 egg whites

2 egg yolks

2 cups whipping cream, divided

White pepper

¼ cup butter

2 cups chopped red peppers

2 cups chopped green peppers

½ cup chopped onion

6 slices eggplant, ¾ inch thick

6 (6 oz.) turkey cutlets, cut from turkey breast

1 cup turkey gravy

¼ cup cranberry sauce

Heat oven to 300 degrees F. Place drumsticks in roasting pan. Roast about 3 hours or until very tender. Cool. Remove skin and bones and pull meat into little strips.

Heat oven to 350 degrees F. Place corn and egg whites in blender container; blend until smooth. Add yolks and 1 cup whipping cream; season with salt and white pepper. Generously grease 6 (2.5 oz.) ramekins; fill with corn mixture. Place ramekins in baking pan. Pour one inch water into pan. Cover entire pan with aluminum foil. Bake 30 to 40 minutes or until cooked in center. Keep warm. Heat 2 tablespoons butter in large skillet; add red and green peppers and onion. Cook until tender; add pulled turkey meat. Cook until heated through. Keep warm. Heat remaining butter in large skillet; add eggplant. Cook until tender and lightly browned. Keep warm.

Place cutlets between sheets of plastic wrap and pound with flat side of meat mallet until about ¼-inch thick. Season with salt and white pepper. Heat grill pan; add turkey. Cook until lightly browned on both sides, about 2 minutes per side. Heat remaining cream in small saucepan until reduced to ½ cup. Stir in gravy; cook until heated through. Place eggplant slice on serving plates; cover with turkey cutlet. Unmold corn timbale; place on plate. Top with pepper mixture. Garnish with gravy and cranberry sauce. 6 servings.

Shrimp and Leeks in California Chardonnay Cream

Chardonnay Cream

1 teaspoon butter
¼ cup chopped shallots
½ cup chardonnay wine
1 cup fish stock*
½ cup half-and-half
½ cup whipping cream
1 teaspoon roux*

1 lb. puff pastry dough
1 egg yolk
2 tablespoons butter, divided
2 leeks, julienned
3 lb. shrimp, peeled and deveined
¼ cup chardonnay wine
2 tablespoons lobster nage*

For Chardonnay Cream, melt butter in small saucepan; add shallots. Cook until softened. Add wine; cook until wine is almost evaporated. Stir in stock, half-and-half and cream. Add roux; reduce heat to low. Simmer 20 minutes, stirring occasionally. Keep warm.

Heat oven to 400 degrees F. Roll puff pastry to ³⁄₁₆-inch thickness. Cut 6 (3½ x 2 inch) rectangles. Place on baking sheet; brush with egg yolk. Bake 15 minutes or until golden brown. Cool; slice in half horizontally. Melt 1 tablespoon butter in medium skillet; add leeks. Cook until tender; season with salt and pepper. Melt remaining butter in large skillet; add shrimp. Cook until shrimp turn pink; stir in wine. Stir to remove browned bits. Add Chardonnay Cream; season with salt and pepper.

Arrange bottom halves of pastry on serving plates; spoon shrimp mixture onto pastry. Sprinkle with leek julienne and cover with top halves of pastry. Garnish with lobster nage. 6 servings.

*See Chef's Notes

Veal Oscar

18 baby carrots, peeled
18 asparagus spears
4 tablespoons butter, divided
3 lb. veal medallions
4 tablespoons olive oil, divided
2 cups demi-glace*
Risotto
12 oz. chunk crabmeat
6 tablespoons Choron sauce

Cook carrots in boiling salted water 5 to 8 minutes or until tender crisp; drain. Cool in ice water. Cook asparagus in boiling salted water 6 to 8 minutes or until tender crisp; drain. Cool in ice water. Heat butter in medium skillet; add vegetables. Season with salt and pepper; keep warm.

Heat oven to 400 degrees F. Place veal between sheets of plastic wrap and pound with flat side of meat mallet until about ¼-inch thick. Season with salt and white pepper. Heat olive oil in two large oven-proof skillets; add veal. Cook until lightly browned on both sides; place in oven. Bake about 4 minutes or until cooked medium well. Remove veal; keep warm. Add demi-glace and remaining butter to pans; bring to a boil. Stir to loosen browned bits. Reduce heat; cook until liquid is reduced by half.

Heat broiler. Divide risotto onto 6 individual oven-proof serving plates. Add veal, 2 oz. crabmeat and three asparagus spears; spread with 1 tablespoon Choron sauce. Broil until sauce is golden brown. Drizzle with demi-glace. Garnish each with 3 carrots. 6 servings.

*See Chef's Notes

Vegetarian Lasagna

12 lasagna noodles
1 tablespoon butter
1 tablespoon minced garlic
2 cups chopped mushrooms
2 cups spinach leaves
¾ cup chopped onion
Grated nutmeg
¾ cup ricotta cheese
¾ cup shredded mozzarella cheese
1 cup béchamel sauce*
6 slices fresh mozzarella cheese
1½ cups tomato sauce*
6 basil leaves

Cook lasagna according to package directions; drain. Cool. Heat butter in large skillet; add garlic; cook until softened. Add mushrooms, spinach and onion. Cook until tender. Season with nutmeg, salt and pepper.

Heat oven to 350 degrees F. Grease individual molds; line with lasagna. Add layer of spinach, ricotta and mozzarella cheese. Cover lightly with béchamel sauce; repeat. Cover tightly. Place molds in baking pan; pour 1 inch water into pan. Cover entire pan with foil. Bake 30 minutes. Remove molds from oven. Heat broiler. Add slice of fresh mozzarella cheese to each serving; broil until melted. Spoon tomato sauce onto serving plates; unmold lasagna. Garnish with basil. 6 servings.

*See Chef's Notes

Sautéed Noisettes of Lamb with Roasted Salsify

12 (3 oz.) lamb medallions

2 cups olive oil

1 teaspoon crushed white peppercorns

2 cloves garlic

1 sprig fresh thyme

1 sprig fresh rosemary

1 sprig fresh tarragon

3 cups whipping cream

3 baking potatoes, peeled and sliced

½ teaspoon minced garlic

1 lb. salsify, peeled and cut into 1-inch pieces

18 baby zucchini

12 cherry tomatoes, peeled

2 tablespoons olive oil

5 tablespoons butter

1 tablespoon chopped fresh thyme

1 tablespoon chopped fresh rosemary

1 sprig chopped fresh tarragon

2 cups lamb jus

Place lamb in container with cover. Add olive oil, peppercorns, garlic, thyme, rosemary and tarragon; mix to coat lamb. Seal container. Refrigerate 48 hours.

Heat oven to 350 degrees F. Heat cream in medium saucepan until it comes to a boil; add potatoes. Season with salt. Reduce heat to low; simmer until potatoes are almost soft. Add garlic; transfer to baking pan. Bake until golden brown. Meanwhile, cook salsify in boiling water 6 to 8 minutes; drain. Chill in ice water. Cook zucchini in boiling water 2 minutes; drain. Chill in ice water. Cook tomatoes in boiling water 30 seconds; drain. Chill in ice water; peel.

Heat olive oil in large skillet. Remove lamb from marinade. Cook over high heat until browned, sealing in juices. Remove; pour off fat. Drain well. Add 2 tablespoons butter to skillet; return medallions to pan. Cook until glazed and desired doneness. Add chopped thyme, rosemary and tarragon. Keep warm. Melt 2 tablespoons butter in large skillet; add salsify. Season with salt. Cook until lightly browned and tender. Remove; keep warm. Add zucchini and tomatoes to skillet; cook until heated through. Season with salt and white pepper. Heat lamb jus in small saucepan; add remaining butter. Whisk to blend.

Arrange salsify on serving plates; top with 2 lamb medallions. Drizzle with lamb jus. Garnish with potatoes, zucchini and tomatoes. 6 servings.

Seared Medallion of Pork with Porcini Sabayon

Marinade

2 cups vegetable oil

1 teaspoon crushed white peppercorns

1 teaspoon caraway seeds

2 cloves garlic

1 sprig fresh thyme

12 (3 oz.) slices pork tenderloin

1 lb. potatoes, peeled and shredded

4 tablespoons butter, divided

1 leek, julienned (green part only)

½ cup whipping cream

1 lb. carrots, peeled and thinly sliced

2 shallots, minced

¼ cup white wine

Porcini Sabayon

1 cup fresh porcini mushrooms, sliced

1 tablespoon butter

2 tablespoons chopped fresh parsley

3 egg yolks

3 tablespoons consommé

1 tablespoon butter

½ teaspoon caraway seeds

2 cups pork jus

1 tablespoon cold butter

Combine Marinade ingredients except pork; mix well. Place pork in container with cover; add Marinade. Toss to coat. Cover; refrigerate 48 hours.

Squeeze moisture out of potatoes. Heat 2 tablespoons butter in large skillet; add ⅙ potatoes. Cook over low heat until brown and crispy on both sides. Repeat; keep warm. Meanwhile, heat 1 tablespoon butter in medium skillet; add leek. Cook 1 minute; add cream. Cook until cream is almost evaporated. Cool; place some on each potato cake. Cook carrots 1 minute in boiling water; chill in ice water. Melt 1 tablespoon butter in medium skillet; add shallots. Cook until softened; add carrots. Stir in wine; cook until carrots are tender.

For Porcini Sabayon, cook mushrooms in 1 tablespoon butter until tender; season with salt and pepper. Stir in parsley. Whisk egg yolks and consommé in top of double boiler; place over simmering water. Cook, whisking constantly, until mixture thickens. Remove from double boiler; keep warm. Stir in porcini mushrooms.

Remove pork from Marinade; pat dry. Heat 2 tablespoons Marinade in large skillet; add pork. Brown quickly on both sides.

Remove from pan; add 1 tablespoon butter and ½ teaspoon caraway seeds. Cook until golden brown. Return pork to pan; cook until medium well. Remove; keep warm. Add pork jus; cook until slightly thickened. Stir in 1 tablespoon cold butter. Place potato cakes on serving plates; add 2 slices pork. Serve with carrots and mushrooms.
6 servings.

Supreme of Chicken in a Hazelnut Crust

6 boneless skinless split chicken breasts

2 sprigs fresh thyme, chopped

1 teaspoon minced garlic

2 tablespoons vegetable oil

1 tablespoon butter

1 tablespoon chopped onion

1 cup jasmine rice

2 cups chicken stock*

Pinch of saffron

Ginger Sauce

1 tablespoon butter

1 tablespoon chopped gingerroot

1 tablespoon chopped shallot

1 cup white wine

2 cups chicken stock*

1 cup whipping cream

Soy/Ginger Reduction

1 tablespoon sugar

2 cups red wine

1 tablespoon gingerroot juice (from grated gingerroot)

1 tablespoon soy sauce

Place chicken in food storage bag; add thyme, garlic and 2 tablespoon oil. Toss to coat; let stand 30 minutes. Heat butter in medium saucepan; add onion. Cook until onion is tender; stir in rice. Cook until rice is coated with butter. Add stock and saffron; cover. Reduce heat to low. Simmer 15 to 20 minutes or until rice is tender.

For Ginger Sauce, heat butter in small saucepan; add gingerroot and shallot. Cook until tender; stir in wine. Cook until wine is reduced to ½ cup, stirring to remove browned bits. Add stock; cook until reduced. Add cream; cook until thickened.

For Soy/Ginger Reduction, cook sugar in small saucepan until it melts and becomes golden. Stir in wine, gingerroot juice and soy sauce. Cook until sauce reduces and is thick.

continued on page 89

Supreme of Chicken in a Hazelnut Crust
continued from page 87

Carrot Emulsion

1 cup grated carrot, blanched

1 tablespoon grated gingerroot, blanched

1 teaspoon minced garlic

2 tablespoons honey

1 tablespoon vegetable oil

1 cup all-purpose flour

3 eggs, well beaten

1 cup grated hazelnuts

1 cup vegetable oil

For Carrot Emulsion, blend carrot, gingerroot, garlic and honey in mini-processor container until smooth. Gradually whisk in oil.

Remove chicken from marinade; coat with flour. Dip in eggs; coat with hazelnuts. Heat oil in large skillet; add chicken. Cook over medium heat, 6 minutes per side, until no longer pink in center and golden brown. Spoon Ginger Sauce on serving plates; add chicken and rice. Drizzle with Soy/Ginger Reduction and Carrot Emulsion. 6 servings.

*See Chef's Notes

Baked Country Smoked Ham in Sourdough Bread Crust

1 (2 oz.) pkg. sourdough starter

3 cups water (105 to 115 degrees F.), divided

3 cups bread flour, divided

1 tablespoon sugar

½ teaspoon salt

4 lb. smoked boneless ham

1 teaspoon dried sage

6 cloves

5 juniper berries

¼ cinnamon stick

Madeira sauce

Dissolve sourdough starter in 1 cup warm water. Stir in 1 cup flour, sugar and salt. Cover; let rise in warm place until doubled in volume. Add remaining water and enough flour to make a soft dough. Knead dough until smooth and elastic, at least 7 minutes. Cover; let rise 1 hour.

Trim ham to nice half-round shape, about 4 inches in diameter. Grind spices together; rub onto ham. Roll out dough to ¼-inch thickness; fold over ham. Press edges to seal. Cover loosely. Let rise 1 hour. Heat oven to 350 degrees F. Bake 45 minutes or until fully cooked and deep golden brown. Let rest 20 minutes. Slice. Serve with Madeira sauce. 6 servings.

Black Bean and Vegetable Enchiladas

3 cups dried black beans

1 tablespoon olive oil

1 tablespoon minced garlic

1 cup julienned green pepper

1 cup julienned red pepper

1 cup julienned onion

1 cup julienned carrots

1 tablespoon fajita seasoning

2 tablespoons chopped cilantro

1 teaspoon ground cumin

1 tablespoon lemon juice

2 cups chopped green onions

1 cup shredded Monterey Jack cheese

1 cup shredded Cheddar cheese

12 (8 inch) flour tortillas

2 cups tomato sauce*

1 cup salsa

1 tablespoon chopped fresh oregano

1 cup sour cream

1 cup guacamole

Cover beans with cold water; let stand overnight. Drain; place beans in medium saucepan. Cover with 2 quarts water. Bring to a boil; reduce heat to low. Season with salt. Simmer 45 minutes or until cooked through; drain. Heat oven to 350 degrees F. Heat oil in large skillet; add garlic, cook until softened. Add green peppers, red peppers, onions and carrots. Cook until tender. Stir in fajita seasoning, cilantro, cumin and lemon juice; mix well. Divide cooked beans in half. Mash one half; add to vegetables. Add remaining beans, green onions and ½ cup Monterey Jack cheese and ½ cup Cheddar cheese. Divide filling onto tortillas. Fold 2 sides toward filling; roll up. Place in greased 15x10x1-inch baking pan. Combine tomato sauce, salsa and oregano; pour over enchiladas. Sprinkle with remaining cheese. Bake 30 minutes or until heated through and cheese is melted. Serve with sour cream and guacamole.
6 servings.

*See Chef's Notes

Old Fashioned Yankee Pot Roast

3 cups red wine

1 cup coarsely chopped celery

1 onion, chopped

2 cloves garlic

2 bay leaves

3 lb. beef brisket or top round roast

2 tablespoons vegetable oil

½ lb. shallots, peeled

2 cups demi-glace*

2 (8 oz.) baking potatoes, peeled, cut into 1-inch cubes

2 cups whipping cream

2 tablespoons butter

1 cup green peas

1 cup corn kernels

Combine wine, celery, onion, garlic and bay leaves in container with cover. Add meat; cover. Refrigerate 48 hours. Heat oven to 375 degrees F. Remove meat from marinade; pat dry. Heat oil in Dutch oven; add meat and shallots. Cook until meat is browned on all sides. Add about 2 cups marinade. Cover; bake 2 hours or until fork tender. Add remaining marinade during cooking. Remove meat and shallots; keep warm. Add demi-glace; cook until reduced and sauce thickens. Add shallots to sauce. Cook potatoes in salted boiling water until tender, about 15 minutes. Drain; add cream. Mash potatoes; season with salt, pepper and butter. Heat butter in medium skillet; add peas and corn. Cook until heated through. Slice meat. Serve meat with gravy, potatoes, peas and corn.
6 servings.

*See Chef's Notes

Teriyaki Salmon

1 cup teriyaki sauce

½ cup soy sauce

2 tablespoons sesame oil

1 tablespoon sugar

1 teaspoon minced garlic

1 teaspoon minced gingerroot

1 teaspoon cornstarch

1 tablespoon water

6 (6 oz.) each king salmon steaks

1 tablespoon butter

1 cup sliced shiitake mushrooms

1 cup sliced oyster mushrooms

1 cup sliced green onions

Combine teriyaki sauce, soy sauce, sesame oil, sugar, garlic, and gingerroot in medium saucepan. Bring to a boil over medium-high heat. Reduce to low; simmer until reduced by half. Combine cornstarch and water; stir into sauce. Stir until slightly thickened; simmer 5 minutes. Remove from heat; cool to room temperature. Place salmon in food storage bag or covered container; add sauce. Seal bag; refrigerate at least 6 hours.

Heat grill pan; add salmon. Cook about 6 minutes or until cooked through but still moist, turning once. Melt butter in medium skillet. Add mushrooms; cook over medium high heat until tender and most liquid evaporates. Season with salt and pepper. Place salmon on serving plates; top with mushrooms. Bring marinade to a boil; drizzle over salmon. Sprinkle with sliced green onions. 6 servings.

Whole Roasted Quail Filled with Delicate Herb Stuffing

Pear Confit

2 tablespoons sugar

1 cup water

1 sprig rosemary

Pinch saffron

2 pears, peeled, cored and diced

1 tablespoon clarified butter*

1 cup chopped onion

1 teaspoon minced garlic

½ cup white wine

1 cup porcini mushrooms, soaked 30 minutes in warm water

2 cups sliced mushrooms, divided

2 cups demi-glace*

1 cup chicken glaze*

12 slices white bread, cubed and toasted

1 cup milk

½ cup whipping cream

1 tablespoon chopped parsley

2 eggs

6 quail, backbones removed

Marsala sauce

Combine sugar, water, rosemary and saffron in small saucepan for Pear Confit. Bring to a boil. Cook until syrup thickens about 15 minutes. Add pears. Remove from heat. Cool. Remove rosemary. Set aside.

Heat butter in medium skillet; add onion and garlic. Cook until softened. Add wine; cook until wine evaporates. Add porcini; cook 5 minutes, stirring occasionally. Add 1 cup sliced mushrooms. Cook until all liquid evaporates. Remove from heat. Add demi-glace and chicken glaze. Cool. Stir in bread, milk, cream, remaining mushrooms, parsley and eggs. Mix well. Season with salt and pepper. Heat oven to 350 degrees F. Fill each quail with about 1 cup stuffing; place on baking sheets; brush with Marsala sauce. Bake 12 minutes or until cooked through. Serve with Pear Confit. 6 servings.

*See Chef's Notes

Broiled Fillet of Chilean Sea Bass with Truffle Butter

Three Potato Roll

Pinch of saffron

6 cups half-and-half, divided

2 lb. potatoes, peeled

1 lb. purple potatoes, roasted and peeled

Grated nutmeg

6 (7 oz.) sea bass fillets

2 tablespoons butter

1 tablespoon truffle butter

Wilted spinach

12 grapefruit segments, room temperature

12 orange segments, room temperature

Lobster nage*

For Three Potato Roll, soak saffron in 2 cups half-and-half. Cook peeled potatoes in salted water until tender. Divide in half. Mash half potatoes using saffron half-and-half. Repeat using 2 cups half-and-half. Mash roasted purple potatoes using remaining 2 cups half-and-half. Season each with salt, pepper and nutmeg. Place aluminum foil on flat surface; line with plastic wrap. Pipe lines of each mashed potato. Lines should be touching. Roll tightly; chill. To serve, slice in ½ inch slices; steam to reheat.

Heat oven to 400 degrees F. Season fillets with salt. Cook briefly on hot grill or grill pan. Place on buttered baking sheet. Brush with butter and truffle butter. Bake 6 minutes or until fish is cooked through and still moist. Serve with Three Potato Roll and wilted spinach. Garnish with grapefruit and orange segments and lobster nage.

6 servings.

*See Chef's Notes

Filet Mignon with California Cabernet Sauce and Gorgonzola Butter

Gorgonzola Butter

½ cup butter

½ cup gorgonzola cheese

1 teaspoon chopped fresh chives

1 teaspoon minced garlic

1 teaspoon lemon juice

1 teaspoon Lea & Perrins Worcestershire sauce

Tabasco sauce

Cabernet Sauce

1 tablespoon butter

1 tablespoon chopped shallot

½ teaspoon minced garlic

1 bay leaf

1 cup cabernet wine

1 cup demi-glace*

½ teaspoon chopped fresh thyme

6 (10 oz. each) filet mignons

For Gorgonzola Butter, whip butter and cheese until very light; stir in remaining ingredients. Pipe roses onto parchment with star tip; or press into small butter molds; chill.

For Cabernet Sauce, melt 1 tablespoon butter in small skillet; add shallot, garlic and bay leaf. Cook over medium heat, stirring often, 6 minutes. Add wine; stir to remove browned bits from pan. When wine is reduced by half add demi-glace. Season with salt and pepper. Remove bay leaf. Add thyme. Keep warm.

Heat grill or grill pan. Season filets with salt and pepper. Grill to desired doneness (5 minutes per side for medium). Serve with Cabernet Sauce and Gorgonzola Butter. 6 servings.

*See Chef's Notes

Spanakopita

3 cups spinach leaves
3 eggs, beaten
1 cup crumbled feta cheese
2 tablespoons olive oil
¼ cup chopped onion
1 tablespoon minced garlic
2 tablespoons chopped
fresh oregano
2 tablespoons melted butter
5 sheets phyllo dough

Heat oven to 350 degrees F. Sprinkle spinach generously with salt; rub into leaves. Tear leaves into small pieces; rinse off salt. Drain well. Add eggs and feta cheese to spinach. Heat olive oil in small skillet; add onion and garlic. Cook until tender. Cool slightly. Add to spinach mixture. Add oregano. Grease an 11x7-inch baking dish with butter. Cut phyllo sheets in half crosswise. Place one sheet in baking dish letting ends hang over the sides; brush with butter. Repeat using 4 more sheets. Spoon filling into dish; fold ends of phyllo over filling. Brush with butter. Place remaining phyllo sheets over top, brushing between layers. Cut 3 or 4 steam vents in phyllo. Bake 25 minutes or until cooked through and golden brown. 6 servings.

Southern Fried Chicken

3 (1½ lb.) whole chickens,
each cut into 8 pieces
1 tablespoon paprika
1 tablespoon chopped fresh
thyme
Vegetable oil for frying
2 cups all-purpose flour

Remove all bones from chicken except wing bones and leg drumstick bones. Combine paprika and thyme; season with salt and pepper. Rub onto chicken; place chicken in container with lid. Cover; refrigerate 4 to 6 hours. Heat about ½ inch oil in heavy deep skillet. Coat chicken with flour. Cook chicken in oil until golden all over and no longer pink in center, about 12 minutes, turning as needed. Serve chicken with gravy.
6 servings.

Baked Fillet of Caribbean Snapper Creole

Creole Sauce

¼ cup vegetable oil, divided

3 cups sliced onion

2 cups sliced green peppers

2 cups sliced red peppers

3 tomatoes, peeled, seeded and sliced

1 teaspoon minced garlic

1 jalapeño chile, minced

1 tablespoon distilled vinegar

1 cup tomato sauce*

2 tablespoons chopped fresh cilantro

2 sprigs fresh thyme, chopped

½ teaspoon crushed black peppercorns

6 (7 oz.) red snapper fillets

¼ cup flour

For Creole Sauce, heat oil in large skillet; add onions, peppers, tomatoes, garlic and jalapeño. Cook until softened; add vinegar. Cook until vinegar evaporates. Add tomato sauce, cilantro, thyme and crushed peppercorns. Season with salt. Cook until flavors are blended, about 15 minutes.

Heat oven to 350 degrees F. Season fillets with salt and pepper. Coat fillets in flour. Heat remaining oil in large skillet. Add fillets; cook until lightly browned on both sides, turning once. Place in 13x9-inch baking dish. Spoon sauce over fillets. Bake 5 minutes or until fish is cooked through. 6 servings.

*See Chef's Notes

Duck à la Orange

2 tablespoons olive oil

3 sprigs rosemary

3 (4 to 5 lb.) ducks

5 to 6 cups chicken stock, divided*

2 oranges

2 tablespoons butter

½ cup chopped carrot

½ cup chopped celery

½ cup chopped onion

1 tablespoon tomato paste

2 tablespoons flour

4 cups chicken stock*

½ cup orange juice

2 teaspoons sugar

2 black peppercorns

3 bay leaves

¼ cup brandy

1 tablespoon black currant jelly

Heat oven to 325 degrees F. Heat olive oil and rosemary in large skillet. Add ducks; seal on all sides. Place in roasting pan. Cook 1 hour or until temperature reaches 170 degrees F. Remove from oven; cool slightly. When cool enough to handle, remove breast bones, backbones and trimmings. Do not remove skin. Reserve duck bones. Place half ducks on baking pan; add chicken stock to depth of ½ inch.

Remove zest from orange; cut julienne strips. Blanch in boiling water. Cut orange into segments; reserve. Heat butter in medium saucepan. Add carrots, celery, onion and duck bones; cook until well browned. Stir in tomato paste; cook 5 minutes, stirring often. Add flour; continue cooking until flour is browned, stirring often. Add chicken stock, orange juice, sugar, peppercorns and bay leaves. Bring to a boil; reduce heat to low. Simmer 30 minutes; strain. Add brandy, orange rind and currant jelly. Remove bay leaves and peppercorns. Keep sauce warm. Add orange segments just before serving.

Heat oven to 375 degrees F. Return ducks to oven; roast until skin is crispy. Serve with sauce. 6 servings.

*See Chef's Notes

Brochette of Beef Tenderloin Fra Diavola

3 lb. beef tenderloin, cut into 18 cubes

2 red peppers, cut into 1-inch squares

2 green peppers, cut into 1-inch squares

2 yellow peppers, cut into 1-inch squares

2 onions, cut into 1-inch squares

1 cup olive oil

8 basil leaves, chopped

1 teaspoon white peppercorns

1 teaspoon crushed red pepper

2 cloves garlic

3 tablespoons olive oil

1 tablespoon minced garlic

2 cups tomato sauce*

2 cups demi-glace*

2 tablespoons chopped fresh basil

1 teaspoon crushed red pepper

¼ cup pitted ripe olives, coarsely chopped

¼ cup pitted green olives, coarsely chopped

Place beef cubes on skewers alternately with vegetables. Combine olive oil, basil, peppercorns, crushed red pepper and garlic. Place skewers in container with cover; add marinade. Cover; refrigerate 24 hours.

Heat 3 tablespoons olive oil in medium saucepan; add garlic. Cook until tender. Add tomato sauce, demi-glace, basil and red pepper. Bring to a boil. Reduce heat to low; simmer until reduced by half. Stir in olives.

Heat grill. Cook skewers to medium doneness about 4 minutes per side. Brush with marinade during grilling. Serve with sauce. 6 servings.

*See Chef's Notes

Desserts

No epicurean adventure is complete without the ultimate indulgence of fresh, crisp berries, snowy whipped cream, luscious chocolate, and of course... passion fruit.

Warm Napa Valley Grape Strudel with Croquant Ice Cream and Champagne Sabayon

Warm Napa Valley Grape Strudel with Croquant Ice Cream and Champagne Sabayon

Champagne Sabayon

3 egg yolks

3 tablespoons sugar

½ cup champagne

1 cup whipping cream, whipped

2 tablespoons white grape juice

2 cups seedless red grapes

½ cup sugar, divided

2 tablespoons raisins, divided

½ teaspoon cinnamon, divided

½ cup cake crumbs, divided

6 tablespoons butter, melted and divided

8 sheets phyllo dough (8 x 8 inches each)

2 cups seedless white grapes

Croquant ice cream**

For Champagne Sabayon, combine egg yolks, sugar and champagne in top of double boiler. Place over simmering water. Cook until thickened, whisking constantly. Chill. Fold in whipped cream; fold in grape juice.

Heat oven to 375 degrees F. Combine red grapes, ¼ cup sugar, 1 tablespoon raisins and ¼ teaspoon cinnamon in small bowl. Combine crumbs and 4 tablespoons butter; divide in half. Using one half of crumb mixture sprinkle on each of 4 sheets of phyllo; stack sheets. Place red grape mixture over crumbs. Carefully roll dough; place seam side down on greased baking sheet. Brush with melted butter. Repeat process using white grapes. Bake 30 minutes or until golden brown, brushing with butter after 15 minutes of baking.

Slice each strudel into 6 slices. Place one slice of each on serving plate. Add Sabayon sauce and ice cream. 6 servings.

**Tip: Croquant is French for crispy. Choose your favorite ice cream with a little crunch.

French Pear Tart

Tart Dough

1 cup butter
¼ cup sugar
1 cup flour
½ teaspoon vanilla
2 eggs

Custard

4 egg yolks
2 eggs
½ cup milk
½ cup whipping cream
¾ cup sugar

3 pears, peeled, cored and thinly sliced
½ cup apricot jam
¼ cup white wine

Heat oven to 375 degrees F. For Tart Dough, combine butter and ¼ cup sugar in medium bowl; mix until well blended. Mix in flour. Beat together vanilla and 2 eggs; add to flour mixture. Mix until dough forms; chill dough 10 minutes. Grease and flour bottom of 9-inch tart pan with removable bottom. Roll dough 1 inch larger than pan; place in pan. Press dough to sides (dough needs to come to rim of pan). Bake 10 minutes.

For Custard, combine yolks and 2 eggs; beat well. Combine milk, cream and ¾ cup sugar; place in top of double boiler. Cook over simmering water until temperature reaches 140 degrees F. Remove from heat; add eggs, whisking constantly. Strain.

Place pears in tart shell. Pour custard mixture over pears until shell is almost full. Bake 25 minutes or until custard is set. Remove from heat. Let stand 30 minutes. Cook jam and wine in small saucepan to form glaze. Brush over tart. Cool completely. Store in refrigerator.

10 servings.

Mango and Coconut Parfait on Lemon Grass Sabayon

3 egg yolks

½ cup sugar

1½ cups light corn syrup

2 cups whipping cream, whipped

1 cup ripe mango purée

½ cup shredded coconut

Sabayon

2 tablespoons sugar

3 egg yolks

1 tablespoon chopped lemon grass

2 tablespoons lime juice

2 tablespoons champagne

¼ cup whipping cream, whipped

2 mangoes, cut into 6 fans

½ cup raspberries

½ cup blueberries

½ cup blackberries

6 sprigs fresh mint

Combine yolks and sugar in small mixer bowl; beat on high until light and fluffy. Bring corn syrup to a boil. Pour hot corn syrup very slowly into egg mixture, beating constantly on high. Continue beating until mixture is cooled. Fold egg mixture into whipped cream. Stir in mango purée and coconut. Pour into 8-inch square parfait mold lined with plastic wrap; freeze overnight.

For Sabayon, combine sugar, egg yolks, lemon grass, lime juice and champagne in top of double boiler. Place over simmering water. Cook until thickened, whisking constantly. Chill. Fold in whipped cream before serving.

Slice parfait into triangles; cut into triangles, place on individual serving plates. Place mango fan on each. Garnish with fresh berries and mint. Serve with Sabayon. 6 servings.

Chocolate Soufflé

5 tablespoons flour
¼ cup unsweetened cocoa powder
½ cup sugar
¼ cup butter, softened
1 cup milk
4 eggs, separated
2 tablespoons Myers rum
2 tablespoons powdered sugar
2 cups chocolate rum custard

Sift flour, cocoa and 3 tablespoons sugar together in small bowl; add butter. Mix until smooth paste is formed; set aside. Place milk and pinch salt in medium saucepan; bring to a boil over medium heat. Whisk cocoa paste into milk; continue cooking until thickened, whisking constantly. Remove from heat; place in medium bowl. Cool to lukewarm. Beat in egg yolks and rum; mix well. Cool completely.

Heat oven to 350 degrees F. Beat egg whites on high speed until foamy. Gradually beat in remaining sugar; continue beating until stiff peaks form and sugar is dissolved. Fold meringue into cocoa mixture. Pipe mixture into 6 (5 oz.) buttered and sugared ramekins. Place soufflé dishes in baking pan; add ¼ inch water to pan. Bake 45 minutes or until just set in center. Dust with powdered sugar. Serve immediately with warm chocolate rum custard. 6 servings.

Poached Apples in Calvados

6 Granny Smith or cooking apples
2 cups water
½ cup Calvados
¼ cup sugar
1 small cinnamon stick
¼ cup toasted slivered almonds

Remove core from apples; peel if desired. Combine water, Calvados, sugar and cinnamon stick in medium saucepan; heat until sugar is dissolved. Add apples. Cook over low heat until apples are tender, about 25 minutes. Spoon liquid over apples occasionally. Remove apples; place on serving plates. Continue cooking liquid until reduced by half. Spoon over apples; sprinkle with almonds. 6 servings.

Apple Hollander

2 tablespoons strawberry jam

1 (10 inch) pie pastry

4 cups thinly sliced apples

¼ cup sugar

¼ cup butter, softened

½ cup almond paste

6 eggs

1 teaspoon vanilla

1 teaspoon almond extract

3 tablespoons flour

2 tablespoons apricot jam

1 cup whipping cream, whipped

Heat oven to 350 degrees F. Spread jam in pie shell. Arrange apples over jam. Beat sugar and butter in mixer bowl on medium for 3 minutes. Add almond paste; continue beating until mixture is smooth. Gradually add eggs, vanilla and almond extract. Continue beating until very light. Fold in flour. Spread batter over apples. Bake 30 minutes or until wooden pick inserted in center comes out clean. Heat apricot jam; brush over cake. Garnish each serving with whipped cream. 12 servings.

Profiteroles Suchard

⅔ cup water
¼ cup butter
½ cup all-purpose flour
2 eggs
⅔ cup whipping cream
2 tablespoons powdered sugar
½ cup melted ganache, cooled*
2 cups chocolate sauce*

Heat oven to 400 degrees F. Combine water and butter in small saucepan; bring mixture to a boil over medium heat. Remove from heat; stir in flour. Return to heat; cook, stirring constantly, until paste begins to leave the sides of the pan. Remove from heat; cool slightly. Beat in the eggs one at a time. Spoon into pastry bag fitted with ¾-inch tip. Pipe 18 walnut-size mounds onto parchment lined baking sheet. Bake 20 minutes or until golden brown. Cool at least 2 hours. Beat cream and powdered sugar until stiff. Beat in ganache. Split bottom of puffs and fill with chocolate cream. Place 3 profiteroles on serving plate. Serve with chocolate sauce. 6 servings.

*See Chef's Notes

Swedish Chocolate Almond Cake

1 cup sugar
1 cup butter, softened
2 tablespoons almond paste
6 eggs
2 egg yolks
½ teaspoon vanilla
½ teaspoon almond extract
2 tablespoons all-purpose flour
1 tablespoon cake flour
2 teaspoons unsweetened cocoa powder
½ cup cake crumbs
2 tablespoons sugar
2 tablespoons water
¼ cup Amaretto liqueur
Ganache*

Heat oven to 350 degrees F. Line 9-inch baking pan with parchment; grease paper. Combine sugar, butter and almond paste in large mixer bowl; beat on medium until almond paste is soft. Gradually add eggs, egg yolks, vanilla and almond extract. Continue beating until very light. Sift together flour, cake flour and cocoa; add with cake crumbs to batter. Beat on low until just mixed. Beat on medium 2 to 3 minutes. Pour into prepared pan; spread evenly. Bake 15 to 18 minutes or until wooden pick inserted in center comes out clean. Cool; remove from pan.

Combine sugar and water in small saucepan. Cook over low heat until sugar is dissolved. Cool; mix with Amaretto. Brush top and bottom with Amaretto syrup. Spread with ganache. Refrigerate until serving. 12 servings.

*See Chef's Notes

Yogurt Cream Cake with Berries

Blueberry Sauce
2 cups blueberries
½ cup red wine
2 tablespoons sugar

1 (1 lb. 2.25 oz.) pkg.
French vanilla cake mix
⅔ cup sugar
4 egg yolks
½ tablespoon gelatin
1 tablespoon cold water
2 tablespoons hot water
1 cup whipping cream
2 cups plain yogurt
1 cup raspberries
1 cup blueberries

For Blueberry Sauce, cook blueberries, wine and 2 tablespoons sugar in medium saucepan over low heat 5 minutes or until thickened. Remove from heat; cool.

Prepare cake according to directions on package. Pour into greased and floured 10-inch round baking pan.** Bake 30 to 35 minutes or until wooden pick inserted in center comes out clean. Cool in pan 15 minutes. Remove; cool completely on wire rack. Meanwhile, place sugar and egg yolks in top of double boiler, set over, not in, simmering water. Whisk constantly until mixture thickens. Remove from heat; cool completely while whipping mixture over ice bath.

In small bowl sprinkle gelatin over cold water. Let bloom 5 minutes. Add 2 tablespoons very hot water. Stir to dissolve. In large bowl of electric mixer, whip cream until soft peaks form. Slowly drizzle in gelatin mixture and continue to beat until stiff peaks form. Mix yogurt and whipped cream; fold into yolk mixture. Cut cake horizontally into 3 layers. Place one layer on cake plate; spread with some yogurt cream. Repeat. Place third layer over cream. Spread top and sides of cake with remaining cream. Top with berries; refrigerate until serving. Serve with blueberry sauce. 12 servings.

**Available at gourmet and cooking specialty stores

Coconut Crepes with Passion Fruit Mousse

1 tablespoon unflavored gelatin

1½ cups passion fruit nectar

1 cup whipping cream

½ cup plain yogurt

Crepes

½ cup cake flour

½ cup bread flour

¼ teaspoon salt

2 tablespoons sugar

2 eggs

2 egg yolks

1 cup warm milk

¼ cup butter, melted

2 tablespoons brandy

2 egg whites

½ cup sugar

Clarified butter*

⅓ cup flaked coconut

Mango coulis

Toasted fresh coconut, mango or oven-dried pineapple

Sprinkle gelatin over passion fruit nectar; let stand 1 minute. Place mixture in double boiler; heat until gelatin is completely dissolved. Remove from heat; cool until slightly thickened. Beat whipping cream in small mixer bowl until soft peaks form. Add yogurt; mix well. Combine cream mixture with gelatin; mix well. Chill until set.

For Crepes, sift together cake flour, bread flour and salt. Add sugar, eggs, egg yolks and milk; whisk until smooth. Stir in melted butter and brandy. Let stand at room temperature 1 hour. To make a Swiss meringue place egg whites and sugar in medium metal bowl. Place bowl in skillet with 1 inch water. Cook over medium heat. Beat on low with electric mixer until mixture reaches 140 degrees F. Increase speed to high; beat until stiff and glossy and mixture reaches 160 degrees F. Remove from heat. Continue beating until mixture is cooled. Fold into crepe mixture. Heat medium non-stick skillet over medium-high heat; brush with 1 teaspoon clarified butter. Pour 2 tablespoons batter into pan; immediately rotate pan until batter covers bottom. Sprinkle with a little coconut. Cook until top appears dry. Run spatula around edge; turn crepe. Continue cooking until bottom is browned. Repeat with remaining batter. Fold crepes into triangles.

Spoon mango coulis onto serving plates. Arrange 2 crepes on each plate. Top with mousse. Garnish with toasted coconut, mango or oven-dried pineapple.

6 servings.

*See Chef's Notes

Poppy Seed and Wild Berry Parfait

1 (1 lb. 2.25 oz.) pkg. devil's food cake mix

Simple syrup

2 gelatin leaves or ½ tablespoon granulated gelatin

2 tablespoons water

½ cup sugar

2 eggs

3 yolks

2 tablespoons poppy seed

2 tablespoons brandy

2 cups whipping cream, whipped

1 cup raspberries

1 cup blueberries

Heat oven to 350 degrees F. Prepare cake according to package directions. Spread batter in two parchment lined 15x10x1-inch baking pans. Bake cake 12 minutes or until wooden pick inserted in center comes out clean. Cool; brush top of one cake with simple syrup. (Reserve remaining cake for another use.)

Soak gelatin with water; set aside. Whisk together sugar, eggs and egg yolks in top of double boiler. Place over simmering water. Cook until temperature reaches 160 degrees F. and sugar is completely dissolved, whisking constantly. Remove from heat; stir in gelatin. Continue whisking until cool. Stir in poppy seeds and brandy. Fold in whipped cream and berries. Line two 8x4x4-inch molds** or individual molds with layer of chocolate cake. Spread with berry mixture. Freeze overnight. Cut into squares to serve. 6 servings.

**A terrine mold is a good choice of mold for this dessert.

Black Forest Cherry Roll

1 (1 lb. 2.25 oz.) pkg. chocolate cake mix

2 cups dark bing cherries, pitted

½ cup sugar

¼ cup Kirschwasser

3 cups whipping cream, whipped

1 cup shaved chocolate

Heat oven to 375 degrees F. Line a 15x10x1-inch baking pan with parchment paper; grease lightly. Prepare cake mix according to package directions. Spread into prepared pan. Bake 12 to 15 minutes or until wooden pick inserted in center comes out clean. Cool slightly. Remove from pan. Roll loosely lengthwise in clean towel. Meanwhile, combine cherries, sugar and Kirschwasser in small bowl; soak 1 hour. Drain cherries. Unroll cake. Brush Kirschwasser mixture over cake. Spread cake with layer of whipped cream. Top with cherries. Carefully roll up using towel. Frost with remaining whipped cream; sprinkle with shaved chocolate. 12 servings.

Blueberry Blintzes

3 cups blueberries

2 cups cottage cheese

1 cup sugar

1 tablespoon grated lemon rind

Pinch of salt

12 crepes

1 tablespoon butter

2 tablespoons powdered sugar

Blueberry sauce or blueberry syrup

Heat broiler. Combine blueberries, cottage cheese, sugar, lemon rind and salt in large bowl; toss gently to mix. Divide filling onto crepes (about ⅓ cup each). Fold crepes into triangles. Spread butter onto baking sheet; add crepes. Dust tops of crepes with powdered sugar. Place crepes under broiler until lightly browned, about 2 minutes. Serve with blueberry sauce or blueberry syrup. 6 servings.

Basmati Crème Brûlée

2½ cups whipping cream
½ cup sugar, divided
1 package unflavored gelatin
½ vanilla bean
½ cinnamon stick
4 egg yolks
1 egg

Basmati Risotto

1 cup sugar, divided
2 cups Basmati rice
2 cups whipping cream
2 cups milk
½ cinnamon stick

¼ cup sugar
¼ cup almonds
Fresh berries or figs

Heat oven to 325 degrees F. Combine whipping cream, ¼ cup sugar, gelatin, vanilla bean and cinnamon stick in medium saucepan; bring to a boil over medium heat. Blend egg yolks, egg and remaining sugar in medium bowl. Add some of hot milk mixture to eggs, whisking constantly. Add warmed eggs to hot liquid. Cook over low heat, stirring constantly, until mixture thickens and coats the back of a spoon. Strain through fine sieve into lightly greased 8-inch springform pan. Place in water bath and bake until barely set in center, about 35 minutes. Cool slightly; refrigerate overnight.

For Basmati Risotto, cook 2 tablespoons sugar in heavy saucepan over medium-high heat until melted. Stir in rice, coating with caramel. Reduce heat to low. Stir in cream, milk, remaining sugar and cinnamon. Cook until rice is tender, stirring often. Remove cinnamon stick. Cool slightly.

Spread over brûlée. Cover tightly with plastic wrap. Refrigerate until serving.

Melt sugar in small skillet; add almonds. Cook until light brown. Pour out onto waxed paper. When cool, crush. Before serving, sprinkle additional sugar on top of rice; caramelize sugar with butane torch or place under broiler until sugar is bubbly. Remove dessert from pan; cut into 8 wedges. Place on individual serving plates. Garnish with berries and praline. 8 servings.

NAUTICA
SPA®

Providing an exquisite little coda to
our voyage, these dishes feature
light and delicate cuisine that
emphasizes freshness and
simple elegance.

Steamed Turbot in Lobster
and Lemon Grass Broth

Steamed Turbot in Lobster and Lemon Grass Broth

1 mango, thinly sliced

1 lemon

1 lime

1 orange

1 lb. carrots, julienned

1 lb. leeks, julienned

2 stalks celery, julienned

2 cups diced tomatoes

2 egg whites, lightly beaten

2 star anise

1 stalk lemon grass, chopped

½ teaspoon peppercorns

1 bay leaf

3 cups cold lobster stock

6 largest outer leaves from 3 fennel bulbs, julienned

2 cups vegetable stock*

3 lb. turbot fillets

Blanched green onions

2 cups fish stock*

½ cup white wine

12 watermelon balls, room temperature

12 honeydew melon balls, room temperature

12 cantaloupe balls, room temperature

6 sprigs cilantro

6 sprigs chives

Heat oven to 200 degrees F. Place mango on parchment-lined baking sheet. Bake about 1 hour or until dry but not brown. Remove zest from lemon, lime and orange. Peel and cut into segments; reserve trimmings. Cut carrots, leeks and celery into julienne strips; reserve trimmings. Combine citrus trimmings, vegetable trimmings, tomatoes, egg whites, star anise, lemon grass, peppercorns and bay leaf in large saucepan. Stir into cold lobster stock. Bring mixture to a boil. Reduce heat to low; simmer 30 minutes or until stock is clear. Carefully strain through cheesecloth. Cook fennel in vegetable stock until tender. Steam julienned vegetables.

Heat oven to 400 degrees F. Trim turbot fillets; shape into 7 oz. rolls fitting small trimmings inside. Tie with blanched piece of green onion. Place rolls in parchment lined baking pan. Combine fish stock and wine; pour over fish rolls. Rolls should be covered about halfway up the side. Cover with parchment paper. Bake until fish is cooked through but still moist, about 10 minutes. Place fennel leaves in serving bowls; top with julienned vegetables. Place fish roll over vegetables; pour about ⅓ cup boiling lobster broth over top. Divide melon balls and citrus into bowls. Garnish with cilantro, chives and mango chips. 6 servings.

*See Chef's Notes

Grilled Baby Vegetables, Soy Vinaigrette

6 baby eggplants
3 baby bok choy
6 baby patty pan squash
6 baby zucchini
6 baby carrots, peeled
¼ cup soy vinaigrette
18 snow pea pods
Carrot Emulsion**

Cut eggplants and bok choy into halves. Heat grill pan. Grill eggplants, bok choy, squash, zucchini and carrots until tender-crisp. Toss with 2 tablespoons soy vinaigrette. Drop snow pea pods into boiling water; cook 1 to 2 minutes or until still slightly crisp. Chill in ice water. Add to squash mixture. Arrange bok choy diagonally on serving plates. Place remaining vegetables across bok choy. Drizzle with remaining vinaigrette and Carrot Emulsion. 6 servings.
**See page 89

Chicken Consommé with Poached Quail Eggs

1 carrot, julienned
1 leek, white part only, julienned
1 celery stalk, julienned
3 tablespoons distilled vinegar
12 fresh quail eggs
4 cups hot chicken consommé
Fresh tarragon leaves

Cook carrot, leek and celery in boiling water 30 seconds. Remove; chill in ice water. Set aside. Bring 2 cups water and vinegar to a boil. Place eggs individually in boiling water; cook 15 seconds. Remove; chill in ice water. Remove from water; pat dry. Trim uneven edges. Place julienned vegetables in soup bowls; top with 2 poached eggs. Cover with hot chicken consommé. Garnish with tarragon leaves. 6 servings.

Pears and Field Greens in a Saffron-Walnut Dressing

1 cup water

½ cup white wine

¼ teaspoon saffron, divided

1 sprig fresh rosemary, chopped

3 pears

Saffron-Walnut Dressing

3 tablespoons vegetable oil, divided

½ cup chopped shallots

¼ cup rice wine vinegar

½ cup walnut oil

6 cups assorted field greens

½ cup chopped toasted walnuts

Bring water, wine, pinch of saffron and rosemary to a boil in a medium saucepan. Peel pears but leave whole; add to saucepan. Reduce heat to low; poach pears about 8 minutes or until almost soft. Do not let liquid boil. Allow pears to cool in poaching liquid.

For Saffron-Walnut Dressing, heat 1 tablespoon oil in small skillet; add shallots. Cook over medium heat until very soft. Add remaining saffron and vinegar. Remove from heat; cool. Whisk in remaining vegetable oil and walnut oil.

Remove cores from pears; cut into thin slices. Divide greens onto serving plates. Arrange ½ pear on greens; drizzle with dressing. Sprinkle with walnuts. 6 servings.

Fantasy of Fresh Tropical Fruit and Berries

1 teaspoon chopped
gingerroot
1 tablespoon water
1 mango, peeled
2 papayas, peeled, flesh
cut into fans
1 cup strawberries
1 cup blackberries
1 cup raspberries
6 sprigs fresh mint

Place gingerroot and water in mini-processor. Process until puréed; strain. Remove flesh from mango; purée with gingerroot. Spoon mango sauce onto serving plates. Arrange papaya and berries on each. Garnish with mint. 6 servings.

Gazpacho Blanco

8 beefsteak tomatoes
1 cucumber, peeled and
seeds removed
1 green pepper, seeds
removed
½ onion
2 cloves garlic
½ teaspoon chopped
fresh thyme
3 cups plain yogurt
3 tablespoons lemon juice
½ teaspoon
Worcestershire sauce
1 cup diced honeydew
melon
1 cup tomato concassé*
Chopped whites of
2 hard-cooked eggs
6 green pepper rings
6 tarragon leaves

Place tomatoes in food processor bowl; process until smooth. Place strainer over bowl; line strainer with cheesecloth. Pour tomatoes into cheesecloth; bring corners of cheesecloth together. Refrigerate; allow to drip over bowl overnight. Liquid will be clear. Place cucumber, green pepper, onion, garlic and thyme in food processor bowl; process until almost smooth. Add tomato water and yogurt. Pulse to mix. Pour into bowl; stir in lemon juice and Worcestershire sauce. Stir in melon. Cover; refrigerate 4 hours or until serving. Garnish with tomato concassé, egg whites, green pepper rings and tarragon. 6 servings.

*See Chef's Notes

Half Papaya Filled with Poached Ocean Scallop

½ cup plain yogurt

2 tablespoons chopped fresh mint

2 tablespoons lemon juice

2 tablespoons lime juice

1 teaspoon grated lemon rind

Hawaiian Pesto

1½ bunches watercress

1 tablespoon chopped cilantro

2 tablespoons chopped fresh mint

1 tablespoon chopped macadamia nuts

1 tablespoon minced gingerroot

¼ cup vegetable oil

1 cup water

1 cup white wine

½ stalk fennel, chopped

½ cup sliced leeks

4 shallots

Black peppercorns

1 bay leaf

24 ocean scallops

3 papayas, cut into halves, seeds removed, peeled

1½ bunches watercress

Grated rind of 1 lime

Combine yogurt, chopped mint, lemon juice, lime juice and grated lemon rind in small bowl; mix well. The dressing should have a coating texture. Chill.

For Hawaiian Pesto, combine watercress, cilantro and mint in food processor bowl; pulse several times. Add macadamia nuts and ginger; process until smooth. Add oil; process to blend.

Heat water, white wine, fennel, leeks, shallots, peppercorns and bay leaf to boiling in large skillet. Add scallops; reduce heat to low. Simmer one minute. Remove from heat; cool scallops in the stock. Place papaya halves on serving plates. Add 4 scallops to each; cover with dressing. Drizzle with pesto. Garnish with remaining watercress and lime rind. 6 servings.

Steamed North Atlantic Halibut Steak with Fresh Herb Vinaigrette

1 cup julienned carrot

1 cup julienned leek

6 (8 oz.) halibut steaks

½ cup white wine

3 tablespoons butter, divided

1 cup fish stock*

2 tablespoons puréed mango

¼ teaspoon cornstarch

1 tablespoon water

6 cherry tomatoes

2 cups hot couscous

Balsamic reduction

12 baby carrots, steamed

6 green onions, cut into sticks and steamed

1 cup herb vinaigrette*

Heat oven to 350 degrees F. Sprinkle bottom of baking dish with carrot and leek; cover with halibut. Drizzle with wine; dot with 1 tablespoon butter. Season with salt. Cover; bake 8 minutes or until cooked through but still moist. Combine fish stock and mango in small saucepan; bring to a boil. Reduce heat to low. Combine cornstarch and water; stir into sauce. Simmer 10 minutes, stirring occasionally. Stir in 1 tablespoon butter. Keep warm. Heat grill pan; add tomatoes. Cook briefly until lightly browned.

Divide couscous onto serving plates; add halibut. Drizzle fish with mango glaze and balsamic reduction. Garnish with baby carrots, green onions and cherry tomatoes. Drizzle with herb vinaigrette. 6 servings.

*See Chef's Notes

Broiled Squab

Vegetable oil for frying

1 potato, peeled and thinly sliced

1 egg white

4 sprigs fresh tarragon

½ cup peanut oil

2 teaspoons crushed juniper berries

1 teaspoon chopped fresh thyme

6 fresh squab

1½ cups red wine

3 tablespoons balsamic vinegar

¼ cup chicken stock*

1 tablespoon vegetable oil

2 cups chanterelles, sliced

2 shallots, chopped

2 tablespoons margarine

½ cup chopped onion

5 kohlrabi, peeled and cut into sticks

½ cup white wine

1 cup whipping cream

¼ cup chopped Italian parsley

Heat vegetable oil to 375 degrees F. Brush potato slices with egg white. Place tarragon sprig onto top of slice; top with second slice. Fry until crisp.

Combine peanut oil, juniper berries and thyme in large container; add squab. Marinate ½ hour. Remove from marinade; truss squabs. Heat oven to 375 degrees F. Heat skillet to very hot; add squabs. Cook until browned on both sides sealing in juices. Place in roasting pan. Bake 14 minutes. Remove legs from squabs. Set breasts aside; keep warm. Roast legs 8 minutes longer; remove. Pour off fat; add red wine and vinegar. Cook until slightly thickened, stirring to loosen browned bits. Add chicken stock; bring mixture to a boil. Strain; keep warm.

Heat 1 tablespoon oil in medium skillet; add chanterelles and shallots. Cook over medium-high heat until tender. Keep warm. Heat margarine in medium saucepan; add onion. Cook until lightly browned; add kohlrabi. Cook briefly; add white wine. Cook until slightly thickened, stirring to loosen browned bits. Add cream; reduce heat to low. Cook until kohlrabi is tender; stir in parsley. Keep warm.

Spoon creamed kohlrabi into center of serving plates; top with squab leg. Bone breast; slice thinly. Place around legs. Sprinkle with chanterelles; drizzle with sauce. Garnish with fried potato slice and fresh herbs.

*See Chef's Notes

Marinated Thai Beef with Pomelo

1 red beet, peeled and julienned

½ carrot, peeled and julienned

½ daikon, peeled and julienned

½ cup soy sauce, divided

2 tablespoons chopped gingerroot, divided

2 tablespoons chopped lemon grass, divided

2 tablespoons plum sauce

2 teaspoons minced garlic

4 green onions, chopped

1½ lb. beef strip loin, cut into thin strips

2 grapefruits or one large pomelo

2 tablespoons peanut oil

¼ cup orange juice

2 teaspoons sugar

3 oz. rice noodles

Vegetable oil for frying

6 cilantro leaves

Place beet in small bowl of ice water. Place carrot and daikon in separate smaller bowl of ice water so they will curl. Reserve. Combine 3 tablespoons soy sauce, 1 tablespoon gingerroot, 1 tablespoon lemon grass, plum sauce, garlic and green onions in medium bowl; mix well. Add beef strips; toss to coat. Refrigerate 2 hours. Thread onto 12 bamboo skewers. Heat grill pan; cook skewers to medium. Remove beef skewers from pan; add remaining soy sauce. Bring to a boil; remove from heat. Keep warm.

Remove zest from grapefruit; finely dice. Set aside. Cut grapefruit into segments over bowl catching juice. Heat oil in medium skillet; add remaining gingerroot and remaining lemon grass. Sauté 2 minutes; add grapefruit segments and juice and orange juice. Cook over medium heat until thickened, stirring often. Remove from heat. Add sugar; mix well.

Fry rice noodles in deep fat until they puff. Remove; drain on absorbent paper. Divide into 6 servings. Place noodles on serving plates; drizzle with soy sauce reduction. Add 2 skewers to each; drizzle with grapefruit (pomelo) reduction. Sprinkle with grapefruit rind. Garnish with cilantro leaf and curls of beet, carrot and daikon. 6 servings.

Sautéed Pheasant Breast Alsacienne

6 (7 to 8 oz.) pheasant breasts, wing bone-in

2/3 cup olive oil, divided

1 tablespoon dry English mustard

2 tablespoons cranberry sauce

1 teaspoon crushed juniper berries

1 teaspoon chopped fresh thyme

2 sprigs fresh rosemary, chopped

4 cups shredded red cabbage

2 cups red wine

1/2 cup orange juice

1/2 cup cranberry juice

1/2 teaspoon ground cloves

1/8 teaspoon cinnamon

1 apple, grated

1 tablespoon margarine

1 tablespoon sugar

6 potatoes, peeled

3 shallots, chopped

1/2 teaspoon minced garlic

1 sprig fresh sage, chopped

1/2 cup raspberry vinegar

1 cup chicken glaze*

Grated orange rind

Place pheasant in container with cover. Add scant 1/2 cup oil, mustard, cranberry sauce, juniper berries, thyme and rosemary; toss to coat pheasant. Cover; refrigerate at least 4 hours.

Combine red cabbage, wine, orange juice, cranberry juice, cloves, cinnamon and apple; let stand 30 minutes. Melt margarine in large saucepan; add cabbage mixture. Cook over low heat 15 to 20 minutes or until cabbage is tender, stirring occasionally. Stir in sugar; season with salt and pepper. Keep warm. Cook potatoes in boiling water until almost cooked through; drain. Cool slightly; coarsely grate. Heat 1 teaspoon olive oil in large skillet; cook shallots and garlic until softened. Add to potatoes; stir in sage. Heat 1 teaspoon oil in omelet pan; add 1/6 potatoes. Cook over medium heat until bottom is crisp and golden brown; turn. Continue cooking until crisp and golden on second side. Keep warm. Repeat with remaining potatoes forming 6 potato cakes.

Drain; pat dry. Heat 1 tablespoon olive oil in large skillet; add pheasant. Cook over medium-high heat, turning once, until desired doneness (4 to 6 minutes for medium). Remove; keep warm. Add vinegar to skillet; cook until thickened. Add chicken glaze; keep warm. Cut each breast into 4 slices. Place potato cakes on serving plates; cover each with 4 slices pheasant. Add red cabbage; garnish with rosemary, thyme and orange rind. Drizzle with chicken glaze mixture. If desired, serve with glazed cranberries. 6 servings.

*See Chef's Notes

Veal Medallions with Lemon Sauce

12 (3 oz.) veal tenderloin medallions

1/2 cup + 2 tablespoons olive oil, divided

2 tablespoons grated lemon rind

1 teaspoon chopped fresh oregano

1 teaspoon crushed peppercorns

1/4 bunch lemon balm, chopped

12 small red potatoes

12 baby carrots with short green stems attached

8 tablespoons butter, divided

3 cloves minced garlic

Lemon Sauce

2 teaspoons chopped galanga root**

1/2 stalk lemon grass, chopped

5 kefir lime leaves, julienned and fried**

1/2 cup white wine

1/2 cup whipping cream

12 shiitake mushrooms, sliced

2 tablespoons soy sauce

1/2 teaspoon chopped fresh rosemary

1/4 cup demi-glace*

Place veal in container with cover. Add 1/2 cup olive oil, lemon rind, oregano, peppercorns and lemon balm; toss to coat. Cover; refrigerate 4 hours. Cook potatoes in boiling water until barely tender; remove. Chill in ice water. Cook carrots in boiling water until barely tender; remove. Chill in ice water.

Heat remaining oil, 2 tablespoons butter and garlic in large skillet. Remove veal from marinade; pat dry. Cook over medium-high heat until medium rare; remove. Keep warm.

For Lemon Sauce, add galanga root, lemon grass and lime leaves to skillet; cook until just softened. Add wine; cook until slightly thickened. Stir in cream; continue cooking until thickened. Strain sauce; add 1 tablespoon butter.

Melt 3 tablespoons butter in medium skillet; add mushrooms. Cook over high heat until tender, stirring occasionally. Add soy sauce; stir until slightly reduced.

Heat 1 tablespoon butter in medium skillet; add potatoes and rosemary. Cook until heated through. Heat 1 tablespoon butter in small skillet; add carrots. Cook until heated through. Place mushrooms on serving plates; top with 2 medallions. Add potatoes and carrots. Drizzle with lemon sauce and demi-glace. 6 servings.

*See Chef's Notes

**Available at Asian grocery stores

Chef's Notes

Culinary magic starts here. These essential recipes are the building blocks for success.

Béchamel Sauce

¾ cup unsalted butter
1¼ cups all-purpose flour
4 cups milk
1 whole peeled onion
4 whole cloves
1 bay leaf

In medium saucepan, melt butter over medium-high heat; stir in flour. Cook 5 to 6 minutes; do not allow it to color. Remove from heat. In medium saucepan heat milk, onion, cloves and bay leaf over medium heat. When milk comes to a boil remove onion, cloves and bay leaf. Slowly add hot milk to butter-flour mixture, stirring constantly. Reduce heat to low; simmer 30 minutes. Strain; season to taste with salt and pepper. 4 cups.

Beef Stock

2 lb. beef bones
1 cup chopped onion
6 quarts water
½ cup chopped carrot
½ cup chopped celery
4 bay leaves
1 tablespoon black peppercorns

Heat oven to 375 degrees F. Place bones in roasting pan. Bake 1 hour or until bones are nicely browned. Add onions; continue roasting until onions are browned. Place water, carrot, celery, bay leaves and peppercorns in 8-quart stock pot; add bones and onion. Scrape any browned bits in roasting pan into stock pot. Bring to a boil over high heat; reduce heat to medium. Simmer 2 to 3 hours or until flavors are developed. Remove from heat; strain. 4 cups.

Chicken Glaze

1 lb. chicken bones
3 quarts cold water
1 cup white wine
1½ cups chopped onion
1 cup chopped carrot
¼ cup chopped celery
¼ cup chopped leek
1 tablespoon white peppercorns
1 bay leaf

Place bones in 4-quart stock pot; cover with water. Heat to a boil over high heat; simmer 5 minutes. Add remaining ingredients. Cook until mixture comes to a boil; reduce heat to low. Simmer 1 to 2 hours. Skim surface periodically. Strain. Return broth to stock pot. Bring to a boil over high heat; cook until reduced by three-fourths. Season to taste with salt and pepper. 1 cup.

Chicken Stock

2 lb. chicken bones
2 tablespoons margarine
2 cups chopped onion
2 cups chopped carrot
2 cups chopped leek
½ cup chopped celery
1 tablespoon black peppercorns
2 bay leaves
1 sprig fresh thyme

Place bones in saucepan; cover with water. Heat to a boil over high heat; simmer 5 minutes. Drain. In 4-quart stock pot melt margarine over medium-high heat; add onions, carrots, leek and celery. Cook until softened; do not brown. Add water, peppercorns, bay leaves, thyme and chicken bones. Cook until mixture comes to a boil; reduce heat to low. Simmer 4 to 6 hours. Skim surface periodically. 2 quarts.

Chocolate Sauce

6 tablespoons sugar
¼ cup unsweetened cocoa
2 tablespoons light corn syrup
½ cup water
⅓ cup semi-sweet chocolate chips, melted

In small bowl combine sugar and cocoa; set aside. In small saucepan combine corn syrup and water; bring to a boil over medium heat. Boil 30 seconds. Add cocoa mixture; cook until sugar is dissolved, stirring constantly; Whisk melted chocolate into hot syrup. Remove from heat; stir gently until smooth. Sauce can be served hot or cold. 5 servings.

Clarified Butter

1 lb. butter

Melt the butter in a saucepan over moderate heat. Remove from heat and skim the impurities on top. Using a ladle, remove the butterfat. Discard the water.

When you heat the butter, the water and most impurities will sink to the bottom since they are heavier.

Creamy Mushroom Sauce

2 cups chicken stock*
1½ tablespoons roux*
4 oz. dried porcini mushrooms
1 tablespoon clarified butter*
¼ cup chopped onion
2 cups sliced mushrooms
1 cup whipping cream

Bring stock to a boil in medium saucepan; reduce heat to low. Whisk in roux; simmer 30 to 40 minutes or until thickened. Soak porcini in hot water for 20 minutes. Drain well; chop. Heat butter in medium skillet; add onion. Cook until onion is golden. Add mushrooms and porcini; simmer 5 minutes. Add chicken veloute; bring mixture to a boil. Season with salt and pepper. Remove from heat; add cream. Keep warm.
*See other Chef's Notes

Demi-Glace

2 lb. veal or beef shin bones
½ cup chopped carrot
½ cup chopped onion
½ cup chopped leek
½ cup chopped celery
3 cloves garlic, chopped
2 tablespoons tomato paste
16 cups water
½ cup red wine
½ teaspoon black peppercorns
1 bay leaf
½ cup chopped tomato
3 sprigs fresh thyme

Heat oven to 425 degrees F. Place bones in large roasting pan; roast 30 to 45 minutes or until lightly browned. Add vegetables and tomato paste. Roast 15 to 20 minutes, stirring occasionally. In 6-quart stock pot combine browned bones and vegetables with remaining ingredients; scrape any browned bits in roasting pan into stock pot. Bring to a boil over high heat; reduce heat to medium. Simmer 4 to 5 hours, skimming frequently. Broth should be reduced to about 4 cups. Remove from heat; strain through cheesecloth. Season to taste. 4 cups.

Fish Stock

2 lb. fish bones
3 quarts water
½ cup chopped onion
½ cup chopped carrot
½ cup chopped celery
1 tablespoon black peppercorns
4 bay leaves

Rinse fish bones in hot water. Place all ingredients in 4-quart saucepan; bring to a boil over high heat. Skim surface. Reduce heat to medium; simmer 20 minutes. Strain. 4 cups.

Ganache

9 ounces semi-sweet chocolate, chopped
1 cup hot whole milk
1½ teaspoons butter, softened

Place chocolate in small bowl. Place bowl over simmering water; stir chocolate until melted. Pour in hot milk. Stir gently to mix; add butter. Remove from heat. Continue stirring until completely cooled and smooth. 5 servings.

Herb Vinaigrette

¾ cup olive oil
¼ cup balsamic vinegar
1 teaspoon chopped fresh basil
1 teaspoon minced red onion
½ teaspoon chopped fresh oregano
½ teaspoon minced garlic

Combine all ingredients in container with tight-fitting lid. Shake well to blend. Season to taste with salt and pepper. 6 servings.

Lobster Nage

1 lobster head
(or shrimp shells)
2 tablespoons butter
½ cup chopped carrot
½ cup chopped onion
½ cup chopped celery
1 bulb fennel, chopped
2 cloves garlic, minced
Black peppercorns
1 teaspoon tomato paste
¼ cup brandy
3 cups water
1 teaspoon cornstarch
1 tablespoon water

Heat oven to 400 degrees F. Wash lobster head; chop. Place on baking pan; roast until browned, about 40 minutes. Heat butter in medium saucepan; add carrot, onion, celery, fennel, garlic and peppercorns to taste. Cook over medium heat until softened. Add roasted lobster and tomato paste. Add brandy; cook until evaporated. Add water; bring mixture to a boil. Reduce heat to low; simmer 3 hours. Strain; chill. Remove lobster butter from surface; reserve. Combine cornstarch with water; stir into broth. Cook, stirring constantly, until thickened. Whisk in reserved lobster butter. Season with salt and pepper. 1 cup.

Roux

8 oz. margarine
8 oz. flour

Heat the margarine in a saucepan over moderate heat (200 degrees F.). Add the flour and cook it over low heat (200 degrees F.), stirring constantly, for about 20 minutes for pale roux; 1 hour for a blonde roux.

For a brown roux: Brown flour in roasting pan in oven at 275 degrees F. for 3 hours (stir frequently). Heat the margarine in a saucepan over moderate heat (250 degrees F.), stirring constantly, for about 20 minutes.

Tomato Concassé

8 cups water
4 lb. ripe tomatoes
½ cup olive oil
1 cup chopped onion
2 tablespoons minced garlic
½ teaspoon salt
¼ teaspoon white pepper
4 bay leaves

In large saucepan bring water to a boil; add tomatoes. Cook 20 to 30 seconds. Remove tomatoes; plunge into ice water. Peel, seed and finely chop tomatoes. In large frying pan heat olive oil until hot over medium-high heat. Add onion and garlic; cook until onion is tender. Add salt, pepper, bay leaves and chopped tomatoes. Reduce heat to medium; simmer 3 to 5 minutes to blend flavors. Remove bay leaves. 4 cups.

Tomato Sauce

2 tablespoons margarine
½ cup chopped onion
¾ teaspoon minced garlic
4 cups diced canned tomatoes
¼ cup chopped fresh basil
¼ teaspoon dried oregano leaves
2 bay leaves
Pinch of sugar

In medium saucepan, melt margarine over medium-high heat. Stir in onion and garlic; cook until onion is tender. Stir in remaining ingredients. Reduce heat to low; simmer 20 minutes, stirring occasionally. Remove bay leaves. 4 cups.

Vegetable Stock

¼ cup unsalted butter
½ cup chopped shallots
1 cup sliced carrot
1 cup sliced celery
1 cup sliced leek
¼ lb. chicken bones, rinsed
6 cups water
¾ cup white wine
12 white peppercorns, cracked

In 3-quart saucepan melt butter over medium-high heat; stir in shallots. When shallots are tender, stir in carrot, celery, leek and bones. Simmer 6 minutes. Stir in remaining ingredients; reduce heat to low. Simmer 30 minutes; strain. 4 cups.

Index

Enjoy the Moment

The Carnival Experience is about celebrating life's many pleasures.

We hope you relish not only paging through these intriguing recipes and beautiful photographs, but also the indulgence of planning and preparing an exceptional meal.

Take your time exploring new stores for the finest ingredients. Don't forget to look for unusual and inventive garnishes. Talk to your wine merchant and discover the best wines to pair with the dishes you've selected. A little taste testing is in order! Polish your best crystal and china to a sparkle; then set the table with mismatched settings for bohemian charm. Visit your florist for tall tulips, exotic lilies, cascades of roses or brightly colored ranunculus. Choose wonderful music to fit the occasion.

Invite a few dear friends for dinner at eight — or have them come early to help prepare and join in the fun. Do most of your cooking in the morning, then set aside the afternoon for a long soak in a hot bath. Emerge refreshed and ready to take on the world! Of course, dine by candlelight. Candles everywhere! Laugh and talk over dinner for hours. Afterwards, a fine brandy or fresh roasted coffee by the fireplace. Relax and savor a moment of true satisfaction.